The Last Word

Other books by Harriet Bridgeman and Elizabeth Drury

Encyclopaedia of Victoriana
The British Eccentric
Beside the Seaside
Society Scandals
Needlework, an Illustrated History
Guide to the Gardens of Britain and Europe
The Connoisseur's Handbook of Antique Collecting (revised edition)

Other books by Harriet Bridgeman

Erotic Antiques
Mechanical Toys (Introduction)

Other books by Elizabeth Drury

The Butler's Pantry Book

The Last Word

EDITED BY

Harriet Bridgeman
and
Elizabeth Drury

With a Foreword by
John Julius Norwich

ANDRE DEUTSCH

First published 1982 by
André Deutsch Limited
105 Great Russell Street London WC1

Copyright © 1982 by Harriet Bridgeman and
Elizabeth Drury

Printed in Great Britain by
Mackays of Chatham Ltd

ISBN 0 233 97474 1

For Ralph and Mary Turton,
Robin and Will Bridgeman
and in memory of
Maurice and Diana Bridgeman

Contents

Foreword

'In lapidary inscriptions', remarked Dr Johnson, 'a man is not on oath.' The same is true of obituaries. It is natural – at least for most of us – to prefer to remember the qualities of our deceased friends rather than their faults. We look back on their generosity, their marvellous sense of humour, their talent for mimicry or playing the piano, the courage they displayed both in the Western Desert and in their last illness; we tend to forget their rudeness to waiters, their appalling halitosis and their habit of putting out their cigarettes in the butter. Indeed, this charitable attitude is not only natural: it is right. If, as Mark Antony pointed out, it is the evil that men do that lives after them and the good that is oft interred with their bones, surely it must be up to us to do what we can to redress the balance.

But this does not mean that the only good obituaries are *good* obituaries, or that the ideal obituary should be nothing more than an elegant bromide. The skilled obituarist, if he knows his job and his subject well – and remember that the vast majority of these compositions are written while their subject is still very much alive – should be able to produce a pen-portrait that will be instantly recognizable, when the moment comes, to friends and enemies alike. As in all good portraits, there will be a certain degree of *chiaroscuro:* not every aspect of a many-faceted character need be given the same intensity of illumination. But the whole man should emerge, to the point where every reader qualified to pronounce on the matter should smile to himself and murmur quietly 'That's him!'

Readers of the pages that follow will not, for the most part, have had the advantage of an acquaintance with the persons described. They will, however, have plenty of opportunities to see how some of the most distinguished exponents of the obituarist's art have been able to steer that delicate course between admiration and adulation, or between honest objectivity and backhanded bitchiness. They will also find the work of less subtle practitioners, those to whom death appears to mean instant canonization and those others for whom the passage of the Grim Reaper is simply an invitation to whet their own sickles. Most important of all, perhaps, they will discover – if they did not know already – that obituaries need be neither sad nor solemn, and that this tortuous, treacherous byway of literature, for all its pitfalls, can occasionally produce its own little masterpiece.

John Julius Norwich

Editors' Preface

The Last Word is about people, ordinary and extraordinary, and how they were described and judged by their contemporaries at the time of their demise. An obituary notice summarizing a man's deeds and character may not necessarily be fair, nor of course does the subject have the opportunity to contest the assessment, but the immediate comment often has a certain truth and poignancy not always to be found in later and perhaps fuller biographical studies. 'When a great man departs from us, what we desire to know about him is not so much what he did, as what he was', wrote the author of an obituary of Charles Dickens (*Macmillan's Magazine,* July 1870). 'It is the same with great generals and great statesmen, as with great authors. Their skill in statesmanship or war has had its effect, and is duly chronicled: but, after a time, we are more anxious to know what the general or statesman was like – what manner of man he was – than to read about his military glories or his civil triumphs.' This can best be written by one who was acquainted with the deceased, or who at least listened to the first-hand descriptions of those who were acquainted with him and was familiar with the attitudes and standards that prevailed in his time.

Apart from their historical value as contemporary accounts, obituaries may be of literary interest. Whether laudatory, critical or simply factual, serious or humorous, the writing of them is an art of its own, and it is worth observing the changes in style and vocabulary that have occurred in the course of time. When it was fashionable to judge men as heroes or villains, and to describe them as such without embarrassment, the tone of the writing might be of unashamed admiration and grief at their passing – or, indeed, of forthright condemnation. When it became undignified to express openly deep feelings concerning another, when in the twentieth century it was accepted that all qualities and all failings can be explained and diminished by understanding a person's circumstances, sentiment withdrew into understatement. The earlier of these collected obituaries are, for this reason, the most surprising today as well as the most obviously revealing. In general they are also the most entertaining.

The selection has been made from a variety of sources; and the reasons for our choice are equally varied. Obituaries of men and women who played an important part in the affairs of their time are understandably of interest – and in some cases the contemporary judgement differs notably from more recent ones. Some of the accounts were undoubtedly flavoured by the political or religious bias of the publication in which they appeared, or, of course, the personal feelings of the writer.

Curiosities are always irresistible and the obituaries published in eighteenth- and nineteenth-century periodicals provide some remarkable instances. Longevity commanded – and perhaps does still – a certain respect, and, since birth dates were not always recorded, there was scope for error and exaggeration. The cause of death was seemingly of particular fascination and, in the days when medical knowledge was slight, the most imaginative pronouncements were made. The gruesome circumstances of an unnatural or accidental death generally lost nothing in the telling, especially when the writer saw fit to add a description of the state of the corpse.

Some of the obituaries, which are arranged chronologically

by category, are not quoted in full. We have exercised our discretion in extracting passages that are especially revealing of a character, his qualities and appearance, his doings and sayings and the manner of his death. Quotations included in the brief introductions are from the same notice unless stated to the contrary. We have reproduced exactly the form of the original writing apart from substituting 'ss' for the eighteenth- and early nineteenth-century 'ff' and 'fs'. Irregularities in spelling and punctuation are not accidental.

The selection ranges from an unsigned lamentation sent to *The Times* by Queen Victoria on the death of her most favoured servant, John Brown, to a colourful appreciation of the stylish career of a famous society beauty. Doctors, lawyers, statesmen and singers, painters, soldiers, millionaires and missionaries: men and women from all walks of life are portrayed in the following pages.

We would like to thank Will Bridgeman for his help in collating and indexing the material, and Dominica Blenkinsopp, Mary-Jane Coles, Margaret Heath and Sarah Irbey for their help in typing the manuscript. We would also like to thank Douglas Matthews, Librarian of the London Library, for guiding us to unlikely sources. The concluding poem is re-quoted from the 1981 *A Christmas Cracker,* with the permission of John Julius Norwich, and to him we are most grateful for writing the Foreword.

Artists and Patrons

When Sir Joshua Reynolds died
All Nature was degraded:
The King dropped a tear into the Queen's ear,
And all his pictures faded.

On Art and Artists by William Blake (1757–1827)

Sir Godfrey Kneller 1646–1723

Kneller, the North German painter whose original name was Gottfried Kniller, was adopted by the English Court on the occasion of his passing through London in 1678. Charles II was about to sit at this time to Sir Peter Lely when Monmouth obtained permission for Kneller to draw the King's portrait at the same sitting. At the first sitting Kneller had not only nearly completed the portrait, but had also obtained such an excellent likeness as to amaze all those present, including the King and Lely himself. His success was assured and from that moment on commissions poured in.

Sir Godfrey Kneller was lessened by his own reputation as he chose to make it subservient to his fortune. He preferred portrait painting for this reason: 'Painters of history,' said he, 'make the dead live and do not begin to live themselves till they are dead. – I paint the living, and they make me live.' Had he lived in a country where his merit had been rewarded according to the worth of his productions, instead of the number, he might have shone in the roll of the greatest masters; but he united the highest vanity with the most consummate negligence of character – where he offered one picture to fame, he sacrificed twenty to lucre.

He painted in an age when the women erected edifices of three stories on their heads. Had he represented such preposterous attire, in half a century his works would have been ridiculous. To lower their dress to a natural level, when the eye was accustomed to pyramids, would have shocked their prejudices and diminished the resemblance. – He took the middle way and weighed out ornament to them of more natural materials.

Criticised by some for his vanity, Pope laid a wager that there was no flattery so gross but his friend would swallow. To prove it, Pope said to him as he was painting, 'Sir Godfrey, I believe if God Almighty had had your assistance, the world would have been formed more perfect.' 'Fore God, Sir,' replied Kneller, 'I believe so.' This impious answer was not extraordinary in the latter.

His conversation on religion was extremely free. His paraphrase on a particular text of scripture, 'In my father's house are many mansions,' was interpreted by Sir Godfrey thus: 'At the day of judgement, said he, God will examine mankind on their different possessions: to one he will say, Of what sect was you? I was a Papist – go you there. What was you? a Protestant – go you there. – And you, Sir Godfrey? – I was of no sect – Then God will say, Sir Godfrey choose your place.'

The Annual Register of the year 1764

Sir Joshua Reynolds 1723–1792

The art critic and poet Cosmo Monkhouse spoke of the 'beauty of his disposition and the nobility of his character', but adds that 'he was a born diplomatist', which goes some way to endorse Mrs Thrale's famous line, 'a heart too frigid' and 'a pencil too warm'. However, his exceptional distinction as a painter and his pleasant urbanity of manner earned for Reynolds a wide circle of friends and admirers during his lifetime and mourners on his death.

Sir Joshua Reynolds was, on very many accounts, one of the most memorable men of his time:— he was the first Englishman who added the praise of the elegant arts to the other glories of his country. In taste, in grace, in facility, in happy invention, and in the richness and harmony of colouring, he was equal to the great masters of the renowned ages. In portraits he went beyond them. His paintings illustrate his lessons, and his lessons seem to be derived from his paintings. He possessed the theory as perfectly as the practice of his art. To be such a painter, he was a profound and penetrating philosopher. In full happiness of foreign and domestic fame, admired by the expert in art, and by the learned in Science, courted by the great, caressed by sovereign powers, and celebrated by distinguished poets, his natural humility never forsook him. The loss of no man of his time can be felt with more sincere, general, and unmixed sorrow.
HAIL AND FAREWELL!

The Scots Magazine, February 1792

Michael Angelo Rooker 1743–1801

Rooker went about the country drawing and painting the places he visited in a way that was so secretive as to invite the notice of the local people. He was a scene painter at the Little Theatre in the Haymarket as well as a topographical artist and when he was dismissed from the post he suffered a 'dejection of spirits' from which he never recovered.

> About this time, 1788, Mr R. began an autumnal pedestrian tour through the most romantic counties of England and Wales, carrying with him an innumerable collection of things for his accommodation. His appearance and reserved manner not unfrequently raised suspicions of his being a spy; and he was several times actually subjected to confinement, till the opinion of neighbouring justices could be obtained, and which, though favourable to our traveller, did not always prove satisfactory to the loyal inhabitants of the place, who had been at some pains to secure him.
>
> *The Gentleman's Magazine,* May 1801

Francis Wheatley 1747–1801

Wheatley worked principally as a painter of scenes of rural and domestic life because, in the opinion of a contemporary, he was prevented by a physical disability from following the more creditable career of a painter of landscapes.

> Francis Wheatley, esq. R.A.; an artist of talents that might have raised him to the highest distinction in the arts, either in the province of landscape or portrait. From very early life, however, he had been subject to attacks of the gout, which, for a long time, disabled him for a great part of the year, and which, for a considerable time before his death, had wholly deprived him of power to pursue his profession. This infirmity, and the consequences to which it exposed him, prevented him from studying Nature as a landscape; and therefore he was obliged, too often, to have recourse to the evanescent traces of memory.

> *The Gentleman's Magazine*, August 1801

Earl of Egremont 1751–1837

Turner was among the many mourners at the Earl of Egremont's funeral, having for some years enjoyed his friendship and patronage. Turner had been given a room at Petworth as a studio, to which the Earl alone was admitted and then only after he had knocked at the door in a pre-arranged manner.

The Earl's benevolence extended equally to his friends and to his tenants and retainers. The *Taunton Courier* reported that the kindhearted Earl on his death-bed had particularly requested that his donations to the poor of the village of Petworth might be continued as usual. The donations on Christmas Eve 'consisted of a liberal supply of meat; and, during the ensuing week, of clothing of every description, as well as bed-linen, to each poor family in the parish, according to their necessities'. Each year he celebrated his birthday with a party in the park at which thousands of the surrounding villagers assembled to eat, drink and be merry.

'The death of the Earl of Egremont', recorded the *Brighton Patriot,* 'will leave a gap in English society which will not be very easily filled up. He was, we believe, almost the only example left of that old English nobility who regarded themselves as the accountable stewards of their own wealth – as the depository of immense riches for the benefit of mankind.' *The Times* described him as 'a noble specimen of the best breed of English gentlemen'.

> The Earl of Egremont was not eminent as a statesman or a warrior; neither illustrious for eloquence nor genius; he was remarkable for one quality alone, and that was immense benevolence. To do good seemed to be his characteristic; and as other men are praised for their figure, or their rank, their wit, or their splendour, the Earl of Egremont was praised, and praised universally, for his generosity. He seemed to delight in giving, as other men delight in accumulating; and to do good was in him the mere instinct of a noble nature.
>
> Fortunately for the Earl of Egremont, and more fortunately for that portion of mankind that inha-

bited the county of Sussex and the neighbourhood of Petworth, he possessed a princely fortune and long life. These enabled him to indulge to the utmost his charities and his gifts, and allowed him to perform a long succession of useful actions to his fellow creatures.

In the early part of his life he was gay and splendid; loved and indulged in expense without extravagance, or without impairing his fortune; but he detested gambling and drinking, and injured his estates and his constitution neither by one nor the other.

Nature had been bountiful to him in form and face. He possessed a good, but not a lofty figure, and his features were regular and handsome. His manners too were easy, simple, and unaffected; and if he possessed the pride which usually accompanies exalted rank and splendid fortune, it was never shown in haughtiness of demeanour or roughness of character.

He never meddled with politics, nor appeared, if we may form an opinion from his conduct, to understand them; he might despise them or he might not; or, which is more probable, he might think that actions are more sincere than words, and that instead of making long harangues respecting the means of making mankind happy, the better way was to do them some immediate and effectual good. He certainly had more to do with the poor than with the rich, and received a greater satisfaction in seeing a thousand hungry persons enjoying a hearty meal at his expense than in making a vapid discourse to famished multitudes respecting the means of existence.

Brighton Patriot quoted in *The Times*, 16 November 1837

Joseph Mallord William Turner
1775–1851

Turner's working habits surprised his contemporaries no less than his paintings themselves. His jolly, 'somewhat sailor-like' appearance was at odds with the disjointed and diffuse manner of conversation that inhibited discussion of his work; he painted at strange hours and not even his patrons and oldest friends were permitted to visit his studio. Fishing was said to be his principal source of relaxation. 'On the occasion of a professional visit to Petworth, it was remarked to Lord Egremont', with whom he frequently stayed, '"Turner is going to leave without having done anything; instead of painting he does nothing but fish." To the surprise of his patron he produced, as he was on the point of leaving, two or three wonderful pictures, painted with the utmost reserve during early morning before the family were up.'

The great secret of Turner's fame was his constant recourse to nature, and his wonderful activity and power of memory. He would walk 20 to 25 miles a day, with his baggage at the end of a stick, sketching rapidly on his way all good pieces of composition, and marking effects with a power that fixed them in his mind with unerring truth at the happiest moment. He was always on the alert for any remarkable phenomena of nature. He could not walk London streets without seeing effects of light and shade and composition, whether in the smoke issuing from a chimney-pot, or in the shadows upon the brick wall, and storing them in his memory for future use. In 1792, when he was eighteen years of age, the Pantheon in Oxford-street was burnt down. It happened to be a hard frost at the time, and huge icicles were seen the next morning depending from different parts of the ruins. The young artist quickly repaired to the spot, and his picture, 'The Pantheon on the Morning after the Fire', exhibited at the Royal Academy in the following May, witnessed the force with which the scene was impressed upon him. In like manner, the burning of the Houses of Parliament, 40 years afterwards was an event that could not escape the pencil of Turner. He repaired to the spot to make sketches of the fire at different points, and produced two pictures, one for the Academy, and another for the British Institution. The latter was almost entirely painted on the walls of the exhibition. Such was his facility at this period of his life, that he would send his canvass with nothing upon it but a gray groundwork of vague indistinguishable forms, and finish it up on the varnishing days into a work of great splendour. At the Academy also, where, as an Academician, he was allowed four such days to touch and varnish his pictures, he was always the first that came on these occasions; arriving there frequently at five o'clock, and never later than six, and he was invariably the last to quit in the evening. He might be seen standing all day before his pictures, and, though he worked so long, he appeared to be doing little or nothing. His touches were almost imperceptible, yet his pictures were seen in the end to have advanced wonderfully. He had acquired such a mastery in early life, that he painted with a certainty that was almost miraculous. Although his effects were imperceptible on a near inspection of the picture, he knew unhesitatingly how to produce them without retiring from his work to test the result. He was never seen, like Sir Thomas Lawrence and others, to be perpetually walking, although his pictures were scarcely intelligible to others except at a particular focal distance. In some of his pictures of this and a later period, ordinary spectators could discover only a few patches and dashes and streaks, seeming almost an unintelligible chaos of colour; but on retiring from the canvas, magnificent visions grew into shape and meaning. Long avenues lengthened out far into the distance, and sun-clad cities glittered upon the mountain, while cloud-illumined space presented itself to an extent immeasurable, manifesting a grandeur of conception and largeness of style that must serve to demonstrate and glorify the genius of the painter to the end of time.

The Annual Register of the year 1851

James Abbott McNeill Whistler
1834–1903

Whistler created an impression in London not only as an artist but as a man of colossal vanity, pugnacity and arrogance. To him, in the words of *The Times,* 'the world was divided into two classes only – the artists and the not artists; and the latter was a class whose chief function was to provide for the wants of the former, to accept in a grateful spirit what the artists were pleased to give it, and to be heartily despised in return'.

He lived 'artistically', provocatively, a celebrated figure in Chelsea in his straight-brimmed hat and long Noah's Ark coat. By his contemporaries he was worshipped or loathed. The memoir published in *The Studio* described Whistler's painting technique (which so much offended Ruskin and caused him to denounce the painting *Nocturne* as 'a pot of paint flung in the public face') and the reasons for his celebrity.

It is by no means an exaggeration to say that for practically the whole of his working career of some five and forty years Whistler was a personality of extraordinary prominence in the art world. His remarkable and erratic genius, his strange and surprising individuality, gained him from the very first an amount of attention far beyond that usually bestowed upon an artist who dares to take an independent line in his professional practice. He never had, like so many other men who have since been acclaimed as masters, to labour in obscurity, and it was by no means his fate to spend the whole or even any considerable part of his life in striving for recognition. At no stage in his career was it possible to overlook him; his work was too surprising in character and his assertion of himself too outspoken for anyone to fail to be conscious of his existence. People who worshipped his productions as evidences of the rarest ability, and people who refused to regard him as anything but

12

a charlatan who made up in impudence what he lacked in skill, quarrelled for years over him, and he had the wit to perceive that this antagonism was for him a valuable source of publicity and to keep it alive by numberless ingenious devices. Few men have had a shrewder appreciation of the uses of advertisement or have known better how to help themselves on by playing cleverly on popular enthusiasms. He made up his mind from the first that he would not be ignored, and so long as his importance in the world was admitted he was supremely indifferent as to what might be the feelings of the general public towards him.

The Studio, September 1903

Auguste Rodin *1840–1917*

Like the Impressionists, the great French sculptor Rodin despised the outward appearance of 'finish', and sometimes even left part of the stone standing to give the impression that his figure was just emerging and taking shape. In disregarding convention by declaring his work finished when he had achieved his own artistic aim, Rodin did much to pave the way for the acceptance of French Impressionism outside the narrow circle of its French admirers.

> Rodin has often been called even by those who admire him, an incomplete artist, but he could conceive more clearly and execute more thoroughly than any other modern sculptor. Conception grew in his mind with execution, and what he had done always seemed to him only a preparation for what he had to do. Hence the fragmentary state of many of his works. They are projects or studies for something greater; they are related to a larger whole which only existed in his mind. One feels that for him sculpture was an art that he was trying to discover and that he was more eager to discover it than to produce masterpieces. Nevertheless, he did produce them and they are the more moving because most of them seem to suggest something finer still than themselves.

The Times, 19 November 1917

Clergymen, Cranks and Converts

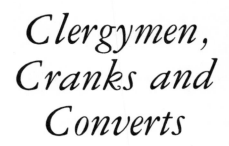

Against her foes Religion well defends
Her sacred truths, but often fears her friends.

The Library by George Crabbe
(1794–1832)

George Whitefield 1714–1770

Although George Whitefield, the evangelist and leader of the Calvinist Methodists, had none of Wesley's administrative genius, he anticipated his career to a remarkable extent. The popularity of his preaching was extraordinary. Almost always extempore, his sermons frequently lasted for as long as two hours, but his charisma was such that he had no difficulty in holding the attention of his audience. Lord Chesterfield, for example, hearing him portray a blind beggar as he tottered over the edge of a precipice, is said to have bounded from his seat and exclaimed, 'Good God, he's gone!' That his death was regarded variously according to the religious stance of the writer can be seen in the following extract from the *Annual Register* which, apparently, felt it its business to show both sides of this particular coin.

As the worth of this truly pious and extraordinary person must be deeply imprest upon the hearts of every friend to true, genuine, and vital christianity, who hath profited by his unwearied labours, little need be said to convince them that their loss is irreparable. – In his public ministrations throughout different parts of Europe, and on sundry visits to British America, he hath for above 30 years, astonished the world as a prodigy of eloquence; by which he was enabled to melt the hearts of the most obdurate and stubborn sinners.

In spite of a constitution of body originally delicate and tender, he continued to the last day of his life to preach with a frequency and fervour that seemed to exceed the natural strength of the most robust. Being called to the public exercise of his function at an age when most young men are only beginning to qualify themselves for it, he had not time to make any considerable progress in the learned languages: but this defect was amply supplied by a lively, fertile, and penetrating genius, by the most unwearied zeal, and by a forcible and most persuasive delivery, which never failed of the desired effect upon his ever crowded and admiring audiences. And though in the pulpit he often found it necessary by the terrors of the Lord to persuade men, he had nothing gloomy about his nature, being singularly charitable and tender-hearted; and in his private conversation chearful, communicative, and entertaining. To the very meanest he was always easy of access, and ever as ready to listen to and relieve their bodily as their spiritual necessities, shewing himself in every respect a faithful steward of the extensive charities he drew from his numerous and compassionate hearers. It ought also to be observed that he constantly and most pathetically enforced upon his audience every moral duty; particularly, industry in their different call-ings, and obedience to their superiors; and in a most especial manner loyalty to our amiable sovereign, never once endeavouring in these distracted times to make a factious use of the great influence he held among his numerous adherents. He was the first of those (since known by the name of Methodists) who endeavoured by the most extraordinary efforts of preaching in different places and even in the open fields, to rouse the lower class of the people from the last degree of inattention and ignorance, to a sense of religion, among whom he hath left an impression, which cannot be soon effaced. For this, and for his other labours, the name of George Whitefield will long be remembered with esteem and veneration not only by his personal acquaintance, by those who were awaked by his ministry, but by all true christians of every denomination whilst vital and practical reli-gion hath a place in the British dominions.

Such is the portrait drawn of Mr Whitefield by the Methodists; the enemies of that sect however, particularly the very learned author of *The Enthusiasm of Methodists and Papists compared,* are so far from admitting his pretensions to an extraordinary portion of sanctity, that they positively pronounce him a most profligate hypocrite; his piety they attribute to avarice; his zeal to pride; and his very humility to ostentation. – They tell us, that during life he was continually boasting of his poverty, yet at his death they talk of his being immensely rich. – This is not all, his late progress to America is set down to the grossest account; an attachment to a woman, by whom he had a child while his wife was living; and it is even added that this child was the first infant ever entered into his orphan-house of Georgia. How far the character on either side may be just, we do not by any means pretend to affirm; the chief particulars of his history we have extracted from his own writings, and as we have given the most flattering eulogium that has been published by his friends, we cannot be deemed partial in mentioning the opinion of his enemies.

The Annual Register of the year 1770

18

Richard Trevor, Bishop of Durham
1707–1771

A munificent patron and a man of considerable learning, the Lord
Bishop of Durham (previously bishop of St Davids) was regarded by
Mr Rotherham, the author of this obituary, and many of his contemporaries in a light approaching idolatry. The degree of eulogy expressed by Mr Rotherham is characteristic of many obituaries written at
this time.

Seldom have so many amiable, so many valuable
qualities, met together in one person, as in the late
Honourable and Reverend Lord Bishop of Durham.
Seldom have virtues and accomplishments been so
happily united.

If we consider him in private life, we shall find
none more worthy of our love; if in public, none that
could more justly claim our veneration and esteem.

He was a master of the best and poorest writers of
antiquity, and his memory was stored with their
finest passages which he applied with propriety and
taste; whilst he felt and communicated the sublimer
beauties of the sacred books with such energy and
warmth of expression, as shewed that their divine
fires touched his heart.

He wore his temporal honours with dignity and
ease. Never were the shining qualities of the PALA-
TINE more justly tempered with the grace of the
DIOCESAN. Liberality, munificence, and greatness
of mind, flowing from one source, were happily
united with meekness, moderation, and humility
derived from the other.

Such was your late benefactor: And such is the rude
outline of a great and beloved character, attempted
by an affectionate, though unequal hand. The
finishing shall be by the hand of an Apostle. For St

Paul, in describing what a Christian Bishop ought to be, hath, in all the principal lines, described what our late lamented Diocesan was.

He was blameless, vigilant, sober, of good behaviour, given to hospitality, apt to teach. He was not given to wine: he was no striker, nor greedy of filthy lucre, but patient, not a brawler, not covetous. He ruled well his own house, having his family in subjection, with all gravity: For, if a man knows not how to rule his own house, how shall he take care of the Church of God? He was neither a novice, nor lifted up with pride: And moreover he had a good report of them which are without, so that he was free from all reproach.

The Annual Register of the year 1771

Mrs Buchan of Thorntonhill *died* 1791

Mrs Buchan of Thorntonhill near Dumfries was the leader of a minority religious group with a misguided sense of her own importance.

Finding she was going the way of all the earth she called together her disciples and exhorted them to continue steadfast and unanimous in their adherence to the doctrine which they had received from her. She then told them she had still one secret to communicate; which was that she was the Virgin Mary, the real mother of our Lord; that she was the same woman mentioned in the Revelations as being cloathed with the sun who was driven into the wilderness: that she had been wandering in the world ever since our Saviour's days, and for some time past she had sojourned in Scotland: that though here she appeared to die, they needed not to be discouraged, for she would only sleep a little, and in a short time would again visit them and conduct them to the New Jerusalem. After she died, it was a long time before her enthusiastic votaries would straighten or dress the corpse; nor did they coffin her until they were obliged thereto by the smell; and after that, they would not bury her, but built up the coffin in a corner of the barn, always expecting that she would rise again from the dead, according to her promise, and conduct them to Jerusalem. At last, the people in the country around, shocked with these proceedings, interfered, went to a justice of the peace, and got an order that she should be buried. So that the famous Mrs Buchan of the West is now lodged in the house appointed for all living.

The Gentleman's Magazine, May 1791

An Aged Negro Woman who Died in Jamaica *died c. 1822*

She was born in Africa. Her parents, she used to say, were remarkably fond of her, being their only child: their little hut was at no great distance from the sea: she was old enough to stroll some way from home; which she did, one day, whilst her mother was engaged. A party of British Sailors, who had been on the watch for such unoffending victims, laid hold of her, and carried her on board their ship. She wept bitterly, she said, for she thought they would soon eat her, as she could not think of anything else they could possibly do with her. The loss of her parents, dear though black, and her fears, so wrought upon her mind, that a fever attacked her, and nearly relieved her from her more degraded oppressors.

After recovering a little, she arrived in Kingston, saw some beef in the market, she said, and said to herself, 'Now I see how they cut up we poor things to sell and eat.'

After a time, she became afflicted. God told her mind, she said, that she was a great sinner: she believed it; and felt that poignant distress, which some convinced and hopeless sinners feel. She went to hear Mr Liele; and by him was told to go to Jesus Christ, which, after some time, she ventured to do. Her own words were – 'Massa, me feel me distress: me heart quite big wi grief; for God no do me no wrong: Him do all good for me – me do all bad to him. Ah, Massa, me heart too full an too hard: me eye no weep; but something so gentle come through me heart, then me eye fill, and God make me feel that him so good to notice poor me, that me throw meself down and weep quite a flood.'

She had a strong desire to read the Bible, but said

22

that she should not live to read it all, but wished to learn two or three verses of some Psalm that suited her. When she heard the first two verses of the Hundred and Third, she said, 'Yes, teach me these: em help to speak God's goodness, for Him so good to me poor thing, that me no know how to tell him so, and him own words best.' She lived to learn them, but she is gone to heaven to repeat them to her good Lord, whom she so greatly loved.

Missionary Register, August 1822

Rev. Henry Hopkins *died 1823*

Whilst in the act of being married to Mrs Smith, a widow, late of Byford, near Hereford, the Rev. Henry Hopkins. On opening the paper and producing the ring, he suddenly fell backwards on the floor, and in less than 10 minutes life was extinct. Although he was extremely infirm, being between 60 and 70 years of age, yet he was first at church, where he waited with great anxiety and perturbation of mind the arrival of the bride, who did not appear till a considerable lapse of time after the appointed hour, which, it is supposed, caused the rupture of a blood vessel, and subsequent death.

The Gentleman's Magazine, Supplement to 1823

Elizabeth Davy *died 1826*

A member of the Unitarian congregation of Crediton, in Devon, Mrs Davy 'exhibited a bright constellation of Christian excellencies'.

> Like that of others, her path was strewn with thorns, but with holy heroism she trampled them down, and under the mellowing influence of sanctified reverses, she advanced in personal holiness and Christian attainments. As years fled with rapidity, setting the Lord before her habitually, she attended conscientiously to her diversified engagements, mingling piety with them; holding daily intercourse with heaven in the closet, and exhibiting to all around a lovely and amiable symmetry of deportment.

> *The Evangelical Magazine*, January 1826

Rev. Rowland Hill *1744–1833*

Minister of the Surrey Chapel in the Blackfriars Road, which was built especially for him in 1783, 'the independent and ambiguous ecclesiastical position which he assumed, as theoretically a Churchman and practically a Dissenter – a Dissenter within the Church, a Churchman among Dissenters – necessarily involved him, especially in the earlier part of his career, in continual polemic skirmishing'. Benevolent in the extreme and an indefatigable evangelist, he preached sermons that were notably unpredictable.

> As a preacher, Mr Hill was extremely unequal, as well as systematically unmethodical; generally rambling, but pithy, often throwing out the most striking remarks, and sometimes interspersing touches of genuine pathos amid much that bordered upon the ludicrous.

> *The Gentleman's Magazine*, June 1833

Rev. Dr Thomas Chalmers *1780–1847*

The life of the Scottish theologian, preacher and philanthropist, Thomas Chalmers, was as interesting as his death. He was the first Moderator of the Free Church of Scotland, his call for independence from civil interference in the Church and the right of parishioners to vote for their minister having led to the Disruption of 1843, when 203 commissioners marched out of the General Assembly and seceded from the Established Church. Whether in admiration of the man or simply aroused by the publication of the curious details of his death, half the population of Edinburgh, it was estimated, attended his funeral.

Great sensation and regret were caused in Edinburgh on Monday by the announcement of the sudden demise of Dr. Chalmers, who attended church on Sunday, and retired to rest at his usual hour in his house at Morningside, near Edinburgh, apparently in perfectly good health. He was discovered by his servant at an early hour on Monday morning sitting up in bed – dead. The legs were crossed over each other, by one of them being drawn upwards to the knee of the other; and betwixt them a basin was firmly retained, which it is supposed the aged divine must have taken into bed on experiencing the first access of the attack, feeling a disposition to vomit. The body was quite cold when discovered.

Douglas Jerrold's Weekly Newspaper, 5 June 1847

Pope Pius IX *1792–1878*

Pope from 1846 to 1878, his was the longest pontificate in the history of the Church. He embarked at first on a series of liberal reforms, but in 1848, the year of revolutions, he fled to Gaëta in the kingdom of Naples. Restored by the French in 1850, he thereafter adopted a reactionary position. The Vatican Council which he convened in 1869 promulgated the dogma of papal infallibility.

Naturally joyous and buoyant as was his disposition, the Pope was, however, subject to fits of sudden irritability, touchy and impatient, and above all things he was resentful of any presumption on his condescension, any approach to disrespect towards his person or dignity. He was easily ruffled by direct and frank contradiction. If it came to any divergence of views, who should know better than the Infallible? His instincts tended to goodwill to all men, and in youth he had friends; but there was something indiscriminate and somewhat instable in his affections, and, after his elevation, he was too full of himself to be capable of much expansion to other men. It was attested to his credit that he was free from the besetting sin of other Popes – he was no nepotist; but it is well to observe that, after his return from Gaëta, it was not he who would not befriend and promote his relations; the estrangement was owing to his brothers, who condemned his reactionary policy, and would not come near him.

The Times, 8 February 1878

Mary Slessor 1849–1915

A panegyric on a notable missionary who, like her friend, Mary Kingsley, belonged to the conventionally unconventional sisterhood of Victorian lady travellers.

No more notable pioneer of the 'woman's movement' has ever existed, albeit in a far-off country and amidst a dark skinned race, than in the person of the late Miss Slessor, whose death in Southern Nigeria completed nearly forty years of unparalleled physical and mental labour in the Christian civilisation of a backward and degraded race.

Miss Slessor's achievements were numerous including the combatting of the ancient custom whereby a large number of slaves or even wives were killed on the death of a great man in order to provide him with a retinue in the underworld. In order to redeem the slaves on one such occasion, Miss Slessor offered in desperation to 'dress the corpse', a necessary preliminary before burial. This she did in a brilliantly coloured dressing gown which had been sent from Scotland for her own personal use, a broad-brimmed straw hat, and a number of large brass buttons. With these she arranged the corpse, distracted the family from their proposed slaughter and won the day.

Her favourite method of enforcing total abstinence amongst a society where drunkenness widely prevailed was to take off her dress and throw it over the rum casks, thus making it 'Egbo' or private property – a practice adroitly gleaned from the rules of a secret society into which the Okoyon had once initiated her.

Her extraordinary physical strength – she was usually her own carpenter and stonemason; the simplicity of her life; her dress – 'just what served to cover her body' – and her food, practically the same as

27

that of the natives; her powerful intellect, utilised in the mastery of numerous baffling dialects, a keen reception of new ideas, and constant omnivorous reading; her fearless courage, her sense of humour and knowledge of humanity; such are some of the shining facets in a Christ-like life, which have caused the name of Mary Slessor to be rooted immovably in the hearts and consciences of the child races of Calabar, whose feet she so loving guided into the pathway of progress and freedom.

The Englishwoman, January 1916

Corrigenda

Life is the art of drawing sufficient conclusions
from insufficient premises.

Note Books. Life. Samuel Butler
(1835–1902)

Sir John Stonhouse

Sir John Stonhouse, not dead, as mentioned from the Papers at the End of last Month, when we had not time to enquire out the Truth.

The Gentlemen's Magazine, July 1733

Captain Murray

Died of their wounds received in the late battle near Tournay, Col. Duroure, Col. Needham of the second regiment of foot-guards, Captain Ogilvie, a son of Alexander Murray of Cringlety, Mr Whitwood, Principal British Engineer.

The Scots Magazine, May 1745

N.B. The report, that Mr Murray, Cringlety's son, died of wounds received at the Battle of Fontenoy, appears to be a mistake.

The Scots Magazine, June 1745

Benjamin Franklin 1706–1790

American diplomat, statesman and scientist, Benjamin Franklin was also one of the heroes of the American War of Independence. His biographers describe his last days as being marked by a 'fine serenity and calm' which is possibly why the French journalists started their inaccurate tittle-tattle. Franklin actually died in April 1790, at the age of eighty-four, from an abcess in the lungs.

The news of the death of the celebrated Dr Franklin wants confirmation, and is generally discredited;

especially as newspapers from New York have been received, dated as late as the 23rd of January, which make no mention of an event which the French advices, copied in some of our prints, have stated as having happened in the middle of that month. The author of the paragraph has also made the venerable Doctor die at an age that he had attained six years ago.

The London Chronicle, 6 March 1788

Sir William Blackett *died 1817*

Mr. Urban,   Jan. 6.

In the Obituary of your Magazine for November last, p. 470, it is stated that Sir William Blackett, bart. of Matson Hall, co. Northumberland, and of Thorpe Lee, Surrey, died on the 27th of October, at Westoe Lodge, co. Cambridge, *aged twelve years,* being born in 1806. – Now the fact is, that he was in his 58th year at the time of his decease. He has left a widow and six children, the eldest of whom, the present Baronet, will be twelve years of age in the ensuing month.

By rectifying this mistake you will oblige one who is nearly connected with this family.

The Gentleman's Magazine, January 1817

Madame Catalani *1779–1849*

Letters received in town from Milan announce the death of this great mistress of song. She expired at her casino, on the banks of Lake Como, on Sunday 26th of last month, in the 61st year of her age.

The Times, 5 July 1841

31

The news of the death of Madame Catalani was false. Letters from Florence of the 25th of June say that this once celebrated singer is in the enjoyment of good health in her native city.

The Times, 16 July 1841

Robert Graves born 1895

Distinguished poet, good soldier and author of arguably the best autobiography in English in this century, Robert Graves is also one of the very few who survived their own obituaries. Severely wounded in France in 1916 he was given up for dead. Unconscious, he was found to be still alive the next day and withstood the agonising journey to hospital. But the formal mechanisms of death in action had already claimed him. The standard letter of condolence by a commanding officer was sent to his mother and the announcement of his death with some biographical details was published in *The Times*. Graves himself was much amused that people with whom he had been on the worst terms during his life wrote of him in glowing terms to his mother. Back in England, recovering from his wounds, he sent the following announcement to *The Times*. It was printed under 'Court Circular' and immediately followed by the information that 'Mrs Lloyd George has left London for Criccieth.'

> Captain Robert Graves, Royal Welch Fusiliers, officially reported died of wounds, wishes to inform his friends that he is recovering from his wounds at Queen Alexandra's Hospital, Highgate, N.

The Times, 5 August 1916

Diplomats and Politicians

And he gave it for his opinion, that whoever could make two ears of corn or two blades of grass to grow upon a spot of ground where only one grew before, would deserve better of mankind, and do more essential service to his country than the whole race of politicians put together.

Gulliver's Travels by Jonathan Swift (1667–1745)

Sir Robert Walpole, Earl of Orford 1676–1745

The politician, Sir Robert Walpole, was not always regarded as uncritically during his own lifetime as he was by the writers of his obituaries. He was ridiculed by John Gay as Bluff Bob in *The Beggar's Opera* but, as Chesterfield was to remark in his letters, 'His hearty kind of frankness had its political value for it seemed to attest his sincerity.'

At London, of an inflammation in his lungs, aged 71, Robert Walpole, Earl of Orford. The following character is given him in some of the pages. 'To all the qualities requisite to adorn the highest station, he added all the virtues which could render a man valuable in private life. In power, without pride; in retreat, without resentment. He lived revered and admired; he died lamented and loved. What would ambition more! and what, would we regard truth, can be said less!'

The Scots Magazine, March 1745

Philip Dormer Stanhope,
Earl of Chesterfield 1695–1773

Politician, wit and author, Lord Chesterfield is best remembered for the letters that he wrote to his natural son, Philip, whose education and progress were the overriding interest in his life.

When questioned shortly before he died on the state of health of himself and his contemporary, Lord Tyrawley, Lord Chesterfield is reported as saying 'Lord Tyrawley and I have been dead these two years, but we do not choose to have it known.' Doctor Johnson censured Chesterfield, confessing that 'he had thought him to be a lord among wits whereas he discovered him to be a wit among lords'. Of his letters to his son, his commendation was merely, 'they teach the morals of a whore and the manners of a dancing master'.

Philip Dormer Chesterfield, late earl of Chesterfield, was born in September, 1695, and received his academical education at Trinity Hall, Cambridge. He left the university in the year 1714, at the age of 19, where, by his own account, he was an absolute pedant. When he talked his best, he quoted Horace; when he aimed at being facetious, he quoted Martial; and when he had a mind to be a fine gentleman, he talked Ovid. He was convinced, that none but the ancients had common sense, and that the classics contained everything that was either necessary, useful, or ornamental. With these notions he first went to the Hague, where, being introduced into all the best company, he soon discovered that he was totally mistaken in almost every notion he entertained. He had a strong desire to please (the mixed result of good nature and a laudable vanity), and was sensible that he had nothing but the desire. He therefore resolved, if possible, to acquire the means too. And this he accomplished, by attentively studying and copying the dress, and the turn of conversation of all those whom he found to be the people in fashion, and most

35

generally allowed to please. Before he came of age, being then stiled Lord Stanhope, he was chosen, in the first parliament of King George the first, for the borough of St. Germain, and in the next for Lestwithiel, both in Cornwall. He tells us himself, that 'he spoke in parliament the first month he was in it, and, from the day he was elected to the day he spoke, thought and dreamed of nothing but speaking.'

His lordship's character, in which, for wit and abilities and especially for elocution or oratory he had few equals, requires a pen or a tongue like his own. An Apelles only can draw an Alexander. His friend Pope has celebrated him, together with the late Lord Bath:

> *'How can I Pulteney, Chesterfield forget,*
> *While Roman spirit charms, or Attic wit!'*

If his morals had been as unexceptionable, he would indeed have been the wonder of his age. His propensity to gaming, and, if one may so say, his gullibility, were most notorious: these, and some other youthful vices, he frankly confesses in his letters, at the same time that he seems unconscious of many other failures in moral duty, particularly of the baseness of seduction and adultery, which even the licentiousness of France cannot excuse a father's teaching and inculcating to his son.

We cannot conclude, without wishing that his lordship had made his will earlier in life, as then he would probably have avoided some glaring inconsistencies which age and infirmities only can excuse in a man of his talents and good-nature. Such are, 1. 'His forbidding his heir to go into Italy, though he had thought an Italian education of the utmost consequence to his son;' and his committing 'the absolute care of his heir's education' to a nobleman who is known to have predilection for that country, and generally resides there. 2. His leaving the mother of his late natural son but 500l. 3. His styling his servants his 'unfortunate friends, his equals by nature' &c. and then leaving them two years wages only; and to two whom he calls 'old and faithful', who had spent their lives in his service, not more than 50 guineas each. 4. His not so much mentioning his excellent lady, whose character ought to have given him a much better opinion of the whole sex.

The Annual Register of the year 1774

Edward Wortley Montague 1713–1776

Member of parliament, author, traveller and son of Lady Mary Wortley Montague, Edward was also a good-looking rake and inveterate
liar. His endless wild exploits, although regarded in a light-hearted
manner by his obituarist, caused serious worry to his mother, and she
came to think of him 'as on the loss of a limb which ceases to give
solicitude by being irretrievable'. In 1751, Sir Horace Walpole was to
write: 'Our greatest miracle is Lady Mary Wortley's son whose
expense is incredible though his father scarce allows him anything.'
The money tended to be squandered on gambling, dress, and jewel-
lery — 'more snuff-boxes than would suffice a Chinese doll with an
hundred noses'.

> The celebrated Edward Wortley Montague, Esq;
> died lately on his return from Venice to England. As
> this gentleman was remarkable for the uncommon
> incidents which attended his life, the close of that life
> was no less marked with singularity. He had been
> early married to a woman who aspired to no higher a
> character than that of an industrious washerwoman.
> As the mariage was solemnized in a frolic, Wortley
> never deemed her sufficiently the wife of his bosom to
> cohabit with her. She was allowed a maintenance.
> She lived contented, and was too submissive to be
> troublesome on account of the conjugal rites. Mr.
> Montague, on the other hand, was a perfect patriach
> in his manners. He had wives of almost every nation.
> When he was with Ali Bey in Egypt, he had his
> household of Egyptian females; each striving who
> should be the happy she who could gain the greatest
> ascendancy over this Anglo-Eastern Bashaw. At Con-
> stantinople, the Grecian women had charms to capti-
> vate this unsettled wanderer. In Spain, a Spanish
> Brunette; in Italy, the olive complexioned female,
> were solicited to partake the honours of the bridal
> bed. It may be asked what became of this group of

wives? Mr. Montague was continually shifting the place, and consequently varying the scene. Did he travel with his wives, as the patriarchs did with their flocks and herds? No such thing. Wortley, considering his wives as bad travelling companions, generally left them behind him. It happened, however, that news reached his ears of the death of the original Mrs. Montague the washerwoman. Wortley had no issue by her, and without issue male a very large estate would revert to the second son of Lord Bute. Wortley owing the family no obligations, was determined, if possible, to defeat their expectations. He resolved to return to England and marry. He acquainted a friend with his intentions, and he commissioned that friend to advertise for any young decent woman, who might be in a pregnant state. The advertisement was inserted very lately in one of the morning papers. Several ladies answered it. One out of the number was selected, as being the most eligible object. She waited with eagerness for the arrival of her expected bridegroom; but behold, whilst he was on his journey, Death very impertinently arrested him in his career. Thus ended the days of Edward Wortley Montague, Esq; a man who had passed thro' such variegated scenes, that a bare recital of them would savour of the marvellous. From Westminster School, where he was placed for education, he ran away three times. He exchanged clothes with a chimney-sweeper and he followed for some time that sooty occupation. He next joined himself to a fisherman, and cried flounders in Rotherhithe. He then sailed as a cabin-boy to Spain, where he had no sooner arrived, than he ran away from the vessel, and hired himself to a driver of mules. After thus vagabondizing it for some time, he was discovered by the consul, who returned him to his friends in England. They received him with a joy equal to that of the father of the prodigal son in the gospel. A private tutor was employed to recover those rudiments of learning which a life of dissipation, of blackguardism, and of vulgarity, might have obliterated. Wortley was sent to the West-Indies, where he remained some time, then returned to England, acted according to the dignity of his birth, was chosen a member, and served in two successive parliaments. His expences exceeding his income, he became involved in debt, quitting his native country, and commenced that wandering traveller he continued to the time of his death. Having visited most of the eastern countries, he contracted a partiality for their manners. He drank little wine; a great deal of coffee; wore a long beard; smoked much; and even whilst at Venice, he was habited in the eastern stile. He sat cross-legged in the Turkish fashion, through choice. With the Hebrew, the Arabic, the Chaldaïc, and the Persian languages, he was as well acquainted as with his native tongue. He published several pieces. One an the 'Rise and Fall of the Roman Empire.' Another on exploration of 'The Causes of Earthquakes.' He had great natural abilities, a vast share of acquired knowledge. He had scarcely a single vice – *for he is dead.* That he had virtues to counterbalance his failings, Omniscience will discover, when weighing them in the scale of merit. Infinite mercy will take care that the beam shall preponderate in favour of his future happiness.

The Annual Register of the year 1776

Hon. Lieutenant-General William
Keppel *died* 1782

Colonel of the 12th regiment of dragoons, ambassador to France in 1754, Keppel

> dived so deep into the councils of that politic court, as to discover the dark designs respecting America, and gave such valuable information to the British court, as enabled his late Majesty's ministers to frustrate the Gallic designs, and to nip their intentions in the bud.
>
> *The Gentleman's Magazine,* March 1782

John William Ward, Earl of Dudley 1781–1833

The Right Hon. John William Ward, as Viscount Dudley and Ward, was appointed Secretary of State for Foreign Affairs in Mr Canning's administration. He was known for the classical elegance of his parliamentary speeches and despatches, for his independent views and a pronounced eccentricity of manner.

Of his extraordinary absence of mind and his unfortunate habit of 'thinking aloud', many amusing anecdotes have been in circulation. It is a fact that when he was in the Foreign Office, he directed a letter intended for the French to the Russian Ambassador, shortly before the affair of Navarino; and, strange as it may appear, it attained him the highest honour. Prince Lieven, who never makes any mistakes of the kind, set it down as one of the cleverest *ruses* ever attempted to be played off, and gave himself immense credit for not falling into the trap laid for him by the sinister ingenuity of the English Secretary. He returned the letter with a most polite note, in which he vowed, of course, that he had not read a line of it after he had ascertained that it was intended for Prince Polignac; but could not help telling Lord Dudley at an evening party, that he was *'trop fin,* but that diplomatists of his (Prince L.'s) standing were not so easily caught.'

The Gentleman's Magazine, April 1833

42

William Wellesley Pole, Earl of Mornington 1763–1845

A rare example of unbridled invective against a harmless, albeit ineffectual, member of a famous family, who was a politician and, at one stage, Secretary of State for Ireland.

From an early period of his career, it was evident to all who knew Mr Wellesley Pole that he was by no means destined to fill so prominent a position in public life as his brothers Richard, Arthur or Henry; nevertheless in his own bustling, active, practical way, he contrived to do a great deal of public business.

One of his earliest speeches in Parliament was delivered in the year 1802, when he seconded a motion made by Lord Hawkesbury, afterwards Earl of Liverpool, for an address to the King approving the definitive treaty of peace. As one of the early efforts of an inexperienced legislator, this speech passed off pretty well, but it contained no promise of future greatness – nothing which the general mediocrity of his talents, as displayed in after life, had the least tendency to falsify.

At no period of Mr Wellesley Pole's life did he manifest Parliamentary talents of a high order: though in the House of Commons he was accustomed to display unbounded confidence in his own judgement; and this habit, combined with other peculiarities, rendered his speeches anything but acceptable to the members of that assembly. Other speakers appeared at times to be under the influence of varied feelings, such as triumph or regret, surprise, joy, disgust or admiration; but Mr. Wellesley Pole was simply angry – angry at all times, with every person, and about everything; his sharp, shrill, loud voice grating on the ear as if nature had never intended it should be used for the purpose of giving expression to any agreeable sentiment, or any conciliatory phrase. It may be true that his unpopularity in the House of Commons became somewhat aggravated by the comparisons which were unavoidably instituted between him and his illustrious brothers but apart from the influence of any rivalry, or the effect of any comparisons, it must be acknowledged that Mr Wellesley Pole was an undignified, ineffective speaker, an indiscreet politician, and a man by no means skilful in the conduct of official transactions.

The Times, 24 February 1845

Earl Russell 1792–1878

'A continental nation, with warm sentiments and easily-moved passions, would, perhaps, judge Lord Russell's public life to be wanting in brilliancy and effect, but Englishmen are not in sympathy with demands like these. In their eyes', observed *The Times*, 'pride wrapped in rigorous reserve and sobriety of expression and demeanour approaching frigidity are important elements in the dignified character of the statesman.'

Sydney Smith, clergyman and favourite among the Whigs of Holland House, made the comment, quoted in Lord Russell's obituary, that a peculiarity of all Russells is that they never altered their opinions: 'They are an excellent race, but they must be trepanned before they can be convinced.' Russell's obstinate trust in his own political convictions he made clear in Parliamentary debate.

His oratorical style was, in spite of many mannerisms and a slightly provincial accent, one of the most effective known in modern Parliamentary history. He was always clear, often incisive, and if he seldom rose far above the commonplace either in idea or expression, his cold dignity was effectually impressive, and his unflinching confidence repelled sarcasms and syllogisms alike. His honest, intellectual contempt for all men who did not hold to the orthodox Whig faith was ingrained, and was hardly disguised by a frigid courtesy.

The Times, 29 May 1878

Léon Gambetta *1838–1883*

Gambetta was President of the Chamber of Deputies and from 1881 to 1882 Premier of France. The most spectacular incident in his career as a statesman was when, as a member of the National Defence Government, he was ordered to help govern the French provinces from Tours and managed to escape from Prussian-besieged Paris by balloon. It began to lose height just as he was passing over the enemy lines until he was almost within range of the marksmen's rifles.

He had previously made a name for himself as a lawyer, initially in 1868 with his bold defence of the republican editor of the *Reveil*, Louis Charles Delescluze. As Gambetta rose to speak, the judge remarked, 'I suppose you have not much to say; so it will hardly be worth while to have the gas lighted.' 'Never mind the gas,' replied Gambetta, 'I will throw light enough on this affair.' His brilliance found vent that day and, spurred on by the laughter produced by his answer, he spoke from first to last without halt.

> A plutocrat once asked Horace Vernet to 'do him a little thing in pencil' for his album. Vernet did the little thing and asked 1000 francs for it. 'But it only took you five minutes to draw,' exclaimed the man of wealth. 'Yes, but it took me thirty years to learn to do it in five minutes,' replied Vernet. And so Gambetta, when some one remarked that he was very lucky in having conquered renown by a single speech, broke out impetuously, 'I was years preparing that speech – twenty times I wanted to deliver it, but did not feel that I had it here (touching his head), though it palpitated here (thumping his breast) as if it would break my heart.'
>
> *The Times*, 2 January 1883

Lord Odo Russell, Baron
Ampthill 1829–1884

Lord Odo Russell was one of the most successful British ambassadors of the nineteenth century. When he died Bismarck remarked, 'England might give a successor to the Ambassador she has lost, but she could not expect to replace him!'

The Press here, without exception, unites in lauding the deceased Ambassador, and in deploring his death as a real loss, not only to England, but also to Germany. The following is a portrait by a clever French writer (by no means popular in Berlin) of the late Lord Ampthill, with which his Lordship once confessed that he felt flattered.

'Gifted with keen wit, remarkable penetration, and exquisite tact, he was a diplomatist of the old school, able to conceal his own thoughts, to discover those of others, to be silent when necessary, and to speak at the right time. Having for some time been Chargé d'Affaires at Rome, his intimacy with Cardinal Antonelli enabled him to acquire a thoroughly Italian subtlety, seldom to be met with in an Englishman. A close observer by nature, he has learnt by experience to observe still more closely; he has discovered how to weigh the characters of men, to discern their weaknesses, and to profit by their meannesses and susceptibilities. He has the wisdom of the Serpent. While apparently open-hearted, he serves his country better than those who govern it. In obedience to English diplomatic tradition, he is the slave of neither Ministry nor Minister. In all Lord Odo Russell's utterances there is the germ of a possible truth which, even where it is not strictly true, can never appear to be a falsehood.'

The Times, 27 August 1884

Robert Lowe, Viscount Sherbrooke
1811–1892

Robert Lowe was elected as a Liberal for Kidderminster in 1852. In the House of Commons he at once fulfilled the high expectations of his contemporaries at Winchester and at Oxford by being 'a valuable ally in debate and a vigorous and harassing foe', in particular in his opposition to Mr Gladstone's Reform Bill. From 1868 to 1873 he held office as Chancellor of the Exchequer and in 1880 he was raised to the peerage as Viscount Sherbrooke. 'In politics, society, or business he was the terror of bores,' and scores of his sharp sayings circulated in Downing Street and Whitehall.

'Let us begin by assuming we are all d——d fools, and now to business,' was his abrupt opening of proceedings on a committee of which X, a fussy bore, vacant and captious, was a member. 'Why quarrel with your natural advantages?' was his query to a friend holding up an ear trumpet to listen to another bore.

The Times, 28 July 1892

The Fair Sex

Here lies a most beautiful lady,
　　Light of step and heart was she;
I think she was the most beautiful lady
　　That ever was in the West Country.
But beauty vanishes; beauty passes;
　　However rare – rare it be;
And when I crumble, who will remember
　　This lady of the West Country?

Epitaph by Walter de la Mare
(1873–1956)

Duchesse de Chateauroux 1715–1744

The Duchesse de Chateauroux preceded Madame de Pompadour as the mistress of Louis XV. Historians often regard her as being responsible for the long war of the Austrian Succession, since she delighted in influencing the King to play Mars to her Venus.

At Paris, aged 29, the Duchess de Chateauroux, one of the French King's greatest favourites. – When the King lay ill at Metz, this lady was discharged from the court, by the advice of the Bishop of Soissons, who, it seems, did not think her a proper companion for his Majesty, when death was looking him in the face. The King's former inclinations, however, returning with his health, the Duchess was again taken into favour.

The Scots Magazine, December 1744

Mrs Brett *died 1753*

The respectable-sounding Mrs Brett is revealed here to have had a stormy past. Mothering Richard Savage was not the way to live it down.

At London, aged above 80, Mrs. Brett, a widow-lady, aunt to Lord Visc. Tyrconnel. This lady was, in 1697, Countess of Macclesfield: but having lived some time upon very uneasy terms with her husband, thought a public confession of adultery the most obvious and easy way of obtaining her liberty. She therefore declared, that the child of which she was then great, was begotten by the Earl Rivers. This declaration answered her purpose; her marriage was dissolved by parliament, and her fortune returned. The child was Richard Savage, celebrated for his misfortunes and his wit; who was by this mother persecuted from the first hour of his life to the last. Of which astonishing conduct a particular account is given in Mr. Savage's life, written by Mr. Samuel Johnson.

Bless'd be the bastard's birth, thro' wondrous ways,
He shines eccentric like the comet's blaze.
– O mother, yet no mother! 'tis to you
My thanks for such distinguish'd claim are due.

The Bastard; a poem; by Mr. Savage.

The Scots Magazine, October 1753

Duchess of Kingston 1720–1788

The Duchess of Kingston's amorous exploits have provided endless interest both to her contemporaries and to later biographers. 'She breathed', said the author of another 1788 memoir, 'in an atmosphere of sighs. Every butterfly fluttered around her.'

> She was a woman, the leading features of whose character are more discoverable from a review of her conduct, than from any delineation in the power of the pen to give. If she might be allowed to know herself, her own description of the mutability of her nature should pass for the truth. Her words were these: 'I should detest myself, if I were *two hours in the same temper.*' What she said, she verified; for she was alternately changing from humour to humour. This instability it was which, in the early part of life, occasioned her to be surrounded more with admirers, than friends; and from the hour of her conviction, to the moment of her death, she had not one friend attached to her from a principle of cordial esteem. The Empress of Russia was much disposed to favour her; but, after the novelty of the meeting was over, there was even too much of sameness in the interviews with her Majesty, to be endured. Those to whom the Duchess showed anything like steadiness, were companions of her own selection, and she was ever sure to err most grossly in her choice.

> *The Annual Register of the year 1788*

Madame du Barré 1746–1793

French adventuress and mistress of Louis XV, Madame du Barré was the illegitimate daughter of a poor woman of Vaucouleurs. Having travelled to London in 1792 in an attempt to raise money on her jewels, she was on her return accused before the Revolutionary Tribunal of having dissipated the treasures of the State, conspired against the Republic and worn, in London, 'mourning for the tyrant'. Her contemporaries, scorning her low birth rather than her vices, attributed to her a malicious political rôle which it was not in her character to implement. They did less than justice to her wit and beauty.

Guillotined at Paris, Madame du Barré, the favourite but extravagant mistress of Louis XV, and supposed to have been one of the richest women in the universe. While in this kingdom, jewels to a great amount were stolen from her house. She was accused before the Revolutionary Tribunal with having entered into a conspiracy against the unity and indivisibility of the French Republic; with having favoured the arms of the enemies of France, by furnishing them with immense sums in the journeys which she undertook to Great Britain, whence she did not return till after the month of March last; with having kept up a correspondence and intimacy with the emigrants; with having lived on terms of familiarity with the English Minister, whose portrait she preserved with great care; with having made a collection of counter-revolutionary works; with having preserved her letters of nobility by burying them, as well as the busts of the Royal Family; finally, the act of accusation charged her with having created great dilapidations in the finances by her unbounded extravagance. Of these charges she was found guilty by the jury of the Revolutionary Tribunal, and condemned to die. The execution of the sentence was suspended on account of Madame du Barré having declared that she could disclose important secrets. It was discovered, however, that the declaration had been made merely for the purpose of delay. The sentence was therefore ordered to be carried into execution. In the evening she was conveyed in a cart to the Place de la Révolution. Her behaviour was by no means firm. The executioner was under the necessity of supporting her in his arms during the whole way. When she arrived at the foot of the scaffold the two assistants of the executioner were obliged to lift her upon it. When they were on the point of fastening her to the plank, she exerted all her strength and ran to the other side of the scaffold. She was soon brought back, and tied. Her head was immediately struck off.

The Gentleman's Magazine, December 1793

Madame Roland 1754–1793

The famous wife of the French statesman, Jean Marie Roland de la
Platière, who almost equalled her husband in knowledge, and in-
finitely excelled him in talent and in tact. Through and with him she
exercised a powerful influence over the destiny of France from the
outbreak of the Revolution until her death. On 8 November 1793 she
was taken to the guillotine, where she bowed before the clay statue of
Liberty, erected in the Place de la Révolution, and uttered the famous
apostrophe, "O Liberty! What crimes are committed in thy name!"'

Guillotined at Paris, aged 46, Madame Roland, wife
of the minister of that name, who lately destroyed
himself to avoid suffering the same fate. She was,
perhaps, the most extraordinary woman that this or
any other age has produced. During the administration of her husband, she was the author of all those
papers signed by him, which, for composition, brilliancy of language, and sentiments of patriotism, are
unrivalled. To the enthusiasm of a spirited reformist
she added a degree of firmness that gave weight to her
decisions, and made her company sought after by all
the *Moderés* of Paris. She had her regular *levées* of
Statesmen, and was consulted as though she were the
Prime Minister of State. — Courteous in her demeanour, and easy in her manners, though her extreme good judgement and sense awed her inferiors
into respectful silence, yet she had those means of
conciliation in her power, that never failed to render
her mistress of the principles and the object of those
by whom she was consulted. Whenever Roland gave
a political dinner, his Lady (who in the prime of life
was considered as beautiful) always presided; for it
was she alone that raised him to that situation which,
at length, proved fatal to this great woman, in consequence of his having attached himself to the
weakest party.

The Gentleman's Magazine, December 1793

Georgiana, Duchess of Devonshire
1757–1806

Daughter of the first Earl Spencer, she married in 1774 the 'first match' of her time, the fifth Duke of Devonshire. Her position in society was accompanied by great charm, intellect and style. In 1784 she canvassed passionately for the return of Charles James Fox to Parliament, exchanging kisses for the promise of votes.

The character of her Grace is not to be classed with any of the ordinary ranks of fashion. Her qualities were of a rare and superior kind. Possessing a mind gracefully modelled as her person, she had stored it with many useful, as well as ornamental endowments. She was well read in the history and polity of all countries; but the Belles Lettres had principally attracted her attention, which she has enriched with some compositions of poesy, that demonstrate a fanciful imagination, and an elegant taste. Though forced into female supremacy by that general admiration which a felicitious combination of charms had excited, and so long remained unrivalled, her Grace of Devonshire found leisure for the systematic exercise of a natural benevolence, which yielding irresistibly, and perhaps too indiscriminately, to the supplications of distress, subjected her to embarrassments that the world sometimes imputed to causes less amiable and meritorious. In a word, she had a heart, which the flattering blandishments of fashion might sometimes beguile, but could never corrupt. The Prince of Wales, who had the highest friendship and respect for her, when he heard of her death, exclaimed, 'Then we have lost the most amiable and best-bred woman in England!!!'

The Gentleman's Magazine, April 1806

Mrs Catharine Abbott 1736–1810

In Paradise-row, Chelsea, after a lingering illness, aged 74, Mrs Catharine Abbott, spinster. In the sweet calm, in the constant and gentle uniformity of this good lady's life, common minds might perhaps perceive little to attract their notice, and still less to excite their approbation and applause; for her wishes were few, her pursuits were humble and unobtrusive, the 'noiseless tenour of her way' was kept in a straight but private path of Christian virtue, and the circle of her very respectable acquaintance was studiously limited. Mrs A. remained single through choice, as we are given to understand: she had many matrimonial offers made her; whether her determination was the result of disappointed affection or not, we stoop not to enquire. She was well calculated to adorn either state.

The Gentleman's Magazine, September 1810

Madame de Staël 1766–1817

A somewhat scornful English portrait of the widely admired lady of literature at the time of her marriage to Baron de Staël, Swedish ambassador in Paris. Critical of her want of the domestic virtues and proper marital regard, it represents her as a self-willed and ardently intellectual character.

The lady was wealthy, young, and though not handsome, agreeable and attractive; she was rather under the middle size, yet graceful in her deportment and manners; her eyes were brilliant and expressive, and the whole character of her countenance betokened acuteness of intellect, and talent beyond the common order. But she inherited to the utmost particle from her father his restless passion for distinction; and derived from the society in which she had lived not a little of that pedantry and philosophical jargon which was their foible and bane. Aiming more at literary fame than at domestic happiness, she was negligent in dress, and laboured in conversation; more greedy of applause from a coterie, than solicitous about a husband's regard; more anxious to play 'Sir Oracle' in public, than to fulfil the sweet duties of woman in private; the wife was cold, and the blue stocking ardent; she spoke in apophthegms to admiring fashion, but delighted no husband with the charms of affectionate conversation: to be brilliant was preferred to being beloved; and to producing an effect upon the many was sacrificed the higher enjoyment of being adored by the few.

The Annual Biography and Obituary of the year 1819

Mrs Maxwell *died 1823*

Wife of the governor of St Kitts, Mrs Maxwell died in child-bed at the age of twenty-six. Universally beloved, her life had been a constant round of benevolence and charity and she 'quitted a world of which she seemed destined to be one of the brightest ornaments'.

Her features and her person were lovely. With the highest polish of manners and address, there were united a simplicity and an unconsciousness of superiority, which spread a charm and a grace around her, that made her the delight of the circle in which she moved. Such exalted virtue, and such sincerity and fascination of manner in the high station which she filled, could not fail to have an influence upon the manners and happiness of the youth of her own sex, whom she attached to her by a grace peculiarly her own.

The Gentleman's Magazine, May 1823

Countess of Orkney 1755–1832

Wife of the Hon. Thomas Fitzmaurice, she was born Lady Mary O'Brien and became Countess of Orkney in her own right. The title, according to the ancient laws of the Scottish peerages, could in the absence of a male heir pass through the female line.

Of her birth the following singular anecdote has been related. The Countess, her mother, was deaf and dumb, and was married, in 1753, by signs. She lived with her husband at his seat, Rostellan, on the harbour of Cork. Shortly after the birth of her first child – the lady now deceased – the nurse, with considerable astonishment, saw the mother cautiously approach the cradle in which the infant was sleeping, evidently full of some deep design. The Countess, having perfectly assured herself that the child really slept, lifted an immense stone which she had concealed under her shawl, and, to the horror of the nurse, who, like all persons of the lower orders in her country, was fully impressed with an idea of the peculiar cunning and malignity of 'dumbies', lifted it with an intent to fling it down vehemently. Before the nurse could interpose, the Countess had flung the stone, – not, however, as the servant had apprehended, at the child, but on the floor, where, of course, it made a great noise. The child immediately awoke, and cried. The Countess, who had looked with maternal eagerness to the result of her experiment, fell on her knees in a transport of joy. She had discovered that her child possessed the sense which was wanting in herself.

The Gentleman's Magazine, January 1832

Elizabeth Fry 1780–1845

Elizabeth Fry is best known for her work in prisons, but she was also responsible for establishing libraries at coast-guard stations around the country, was a faithful and diligent distributor of religious tracts, and founded a committee of ladies to help the homeless of London. She was persuaded from early in her life that 'Christianity, in its practical and vital power, was the only true source of a radical renovation of character'. She is said to have gone about her work 'at an easy, steady pace, and was never ruffled, never in a hurry'.

At an early period of her life in London, she was informed of the terrible condition of the female prisoners in Newgate. The part of the prison allotted to them was a scene of the wildest disorder. Swearing, drinking, gambling, and fighting, were their only employments; filth and corruption prevailed on every side. Notwithstanding the warnings of the turnkeys, that her purse and watch, and even her life, would be endangered, she resolved to go in without any protection, and to face this disorganized multitude. After being locked up with them, she addressed them with her usual dignity, power, and gentleness; soon calmed their fury, and fixed their attention, and then proposed to them a variety of rules for the regulation of their conduct, to which, after her kind and lucid explanations, they all gave a hearty consent. Her visits were repeated again and again; and with the assistance of a committee of ladies, which she had formed for the purpose, she soon brought her rules to bear upon the poor degraded criminals. Within a very short time the whole scene was marvellously changed. Like the maniac of Gennesaret, from whom the legion of devils had been cast out, these once wild and wretched creatures were seen neatly clothed, busily employed, arranged under the care of monitors, with a matron at the head of them, and, comparatively speaking, in their right mind.

Every morning they were assembled in one of the wards of the prison, when a chapter of Scripture was read aloud in their hearing, either by the matron, or by one of the visiting ladies. On one particular morning of the week it was Elizabeth Fry's regular practice to attend on these occasions, and to read the Bible herself to the prisoners. This office she performed with peculiar power and sweetness. The appropriate modulations of her deeply toned voice gave great effect to her reading, and the practical comments which she often added, after a solemn pause of silence, and sometimes a melodious prayer in conclusion, were the frequent means, under Divine influence, of melting the hearts of all present. The prison was open, on the appointed morning, to any visitors whom she chose to admit: and her readings were attended by a multitude of persons, both English and foreign, including many of high rank and station in the world, who were all anxious to witness this extraordinary scene of order and reformation.

Norfolk News, 25 October 1845

Marguerite, Countess of Blessington, 1789–1849

Daughter of a dissolute Irish newspaper proprietor and dandy known as 'Shiver-the-Frills' or 'Bean Power', Marguerite was first married to Captain Maurice Farmer. He died in 1817 by falling from a window in the King's Bench prison during a drunken orgy. She married the Earl of Blessington in the following year.

> There can now, perhaps, be no great harm in stating that, between her widowhood and her marriage with the Earl, she was living under the protection of a gallant admirer, one Captain Jenkins, or some such name, between whom and her ladyship she divided her favours; but, the former proposing marriage, she told the latter she would prefer being made a lady as well as merely an honest woman, and the easy-going peer made her both, presenting her with a ring and a coronet at one and the same time, and with a substantial remembrance in his will.

> *The Gentleman's Magazine*, August 1849

Freaks and Eccentrics

England is the paradise of individuality, eccentricity, heresy, anomalies, hobbies and humours.

The British Character by George Santayana (1863–1952)

Mrs Newberry 1699–1732

The wife of Walter Newberry, merchant of Gracechurch Street, in the 33rd year of her age, of the Dropsy, for which from the Year 1728 she had been tapped 57 times, and had taken from her 240 gallons of water.

The Gentleman's Magazine, May 1732

Christopher Cole *died* 1737

The latter end of last Month,—Mr. Christ. Cole, at Bristol, an old Salt-officer: He was very particular as to his way of life: his bed was never made, or shook up, so that it seemed as if a cavity had been carved out to fit it in one posture; his room was seldom visited without urgent necessity, and his Money hid in several parts of it for fear of thieves; Cabbage, and other Greens, he would not suffer to be wash'd, but put into the Pot as gather'd, and taken out when warm, because the Crimpness should not be taken off; he had a blue Jug, stopp'd with a cork, out of which no person drank but himself; was always very positive; and seemed to have a particular care to prevent his Family from sharing the least benefit of his Estate; he left 1100 l. to the Charity-School at Henbury, in the County of Gloucester, where he had his education.

The Gentleman's Magazine, April 1737

Anon

Died in the Parish of St. John's, near the City of Worcester, a poor woman in the 85th Year of her age, having had 4 husbands, and 15 children. In her 80th Year she fell into an Ascites or Dropsy of the Abdomen, which was so dilated that she could not rise out of her bed without assistance; she made her Application (at last) to an eminent and charitable surgeon at Worcester who in August 1733, tapped her, and from thence to the 29th of June following perform'd that operation upon her 32 times. In which several tappings were extracted 342 Quarts of Water; and from the 29th June, 1734 to the 12th of August 1735, she continued without tapping in such a good state of Health, that she was able to walk about by the Assistance of one stick only; but about the latter end of July 1735, she began to fill again, and upon the 12th of August she was tapp'd and continu'd to fill as to require the operation once every Month or 6 weeks, until about a quarter of a Year before she died, in which time she was tapped once every fortnight or 3 weeks, and from first and last hath been Tapped 50 times; and had extracted from her in all 116 gallons of Water.

The Gentleman's Magazine, September 1737

Roger Gill *died* 1767

At Winbourn, Dorset, Roger Gill, shoe-maker and one of the singing men of that place, aged about 67; remarkable for chewing his meat, or cud, twice over, as an ox, sheep, or cow. He seldom made any breakfast in his latter days; he generally dined about twelve or one o'clock; eat pretty heartily and quickly, without much chewing or mastification. He never drank with his dinner, but afterwards about a pint of such malt-liquor as he could get; but no sort of spirituous liquor in any shape, except a little punch, but never much cared for that. He usually began his second chewing about a quarter, or half an hour, sometimes later, after dinner; when every morsel came up successively, sweeter and sweeter to the taste. Sometimes a morsel would prove offensive and crude, in which case he spit it out. The chewing continued usually about an hour or more, and sometimes would leave him a little while, in which case he would be sick at stomach, troubled with the heart-burn, foul breath, etc. Smoking tobacco would sometimes stop his chewing, but was never attended with any ill consequence. But on the 10th of June last this faculty entirely left him; and the poor man remained in great tortures till the time of his death.

The Scots Magazine, September 1767

Anon

Suddenly at the sign of Clifford's Tower, upon Pease-holm Green, in York, where she had been exhibited to the curious for a few days past, the surprising gigantic Worcestershire girl. This child was only five years old in June last, was very beautiful and handsomely made, and quite active and agreeable, although she was four feet in height, four feet two inches round the breast, four feet six inches round the hips, and round each leg eighteen inches. She weighed near two hundred weight, and was in every respect well proportioned.

The Scots Magazine, November 1788

Mary Watts *died 1792*

An extreme example of lethargy in the fairer sex.

At Fordingbridge, Hants, Mary Watts, a poor old woman whose lethargic habit of body had for three years been extraordinary, and had lately so considerably increased, that she would sleep a week, a fortnight, and sometimes a month, or more, which she considered but as a day. Her son, a weaver, with whom she lived, was accustomed to watch her very attentively, and his usual method of awaking her from her torpor, was by putting food into her mouth. When awoke, she would partake of a small aliment, chiefly liquid, and quickly fall into the same state again. Many efforts were often in vain made to rouse her. She awoke about three hours before her death, and continued awake, apparently in good health and spirits, till the moment of her dissolution.

The Gentleman's Magazine, February 1792

William Lewis *died* 1793

At Beaumaris, Wm. Lewis, esq., of Llandisman, in the act of drinking a cup of Welsh ale, containing about a wine quart called a *tumbler*. He made it a rule, every morning of his life, to read so many chapters in the Bible, and in the evening, as a digestion of his morning study, to drink full eight gallons of ale. It is calculated that in his life-time he must have drunk a sufficient quantity to float a 74 gun ship. His size was astonishing; it is supposed the diameter of his body was no less than two yards. He weighed forty stone. He died in his parlour; a lucky circumstance, as it would have been almost impossible to have got him down stairs; as it was, it was found necessary to have a machine, in form of a crane, to lift him on a carriage, and afterwards to have the same brought into the church-yard to let him down into his grave. He went by the name of the King of Spain, and his family by the different titles of Prince, Infanta etc., but from what circumstance we know not.

The Gentleman's Magazine, May 1793

Edmund Mason *died 1801*

At Leominster, in Herefordshire, Edmund Mason, by birth a gentleman, and remarkable for being, in spirit, integrity, disorder of imagination, and even a ray of intellectual ability, the living representative of the inimitable hero of Cervantes. Though perfectly harmless, he was constantly accoutred in arms. He fancied himself the greatest general of the age; related deeds, achieved by his arm in battle, which no other mortal could equal; believed that kings and emperors had vied in conferring on him every imaginable title and badge of honour. Mason supposed, that he had enjoyed the confidential friendship and admiration of the late great Frederick of Prussia. From his foreign correspondence, he told that immense remittances were sent for the support of his dignity; yet he was ever without money – from the difficulty, as he said, of cashing bills of exchange for millions. He was fond of musick. He had a favourite Ramthus, equal in height of bone and scantiness, to Rosinante, who he thought could outstrip the swiftest race-horse on the turf. He was decorous and dignified in manners, cleanly in his person, temperate in his diet. In love with the fancied princess of some undiscovered land, he would not suffer one of the fair sex about him to touch, even his little finger. His bed was a roomy wooden chest, from which his musket was constantly levelled. He was in his later years confined; but the confinement was reconciled to his mind, by the persuasion that he resided in it as the governor of the castle.

The Gentleman's Magazine, March 1801

Theodore Hook 1788–1841

Hook was a novelist, miscellaneous writer, editor of the outspoken journal *John Bull* and bankrupt, whose company was much sought after in the dining rooms and drawing rooms of fashionable society. A brilliant extempore pianist and singer of ballads, a mimic and story-teller, the real farce was his own life: 'It was one uninterrupted succession of boisterous buffooneries.' In 1809 he perpetrated the most spectacular of his practical jokes, the Berners Street Hoax.

In walking down that street one day his companion called his attention to the particularly neat and mod-est appearance of a house, the residence, as appeared from the door-plate, of some decent shop-keeper's widow. 'I'll lay you a guinea,' said Theodore, 'that in one week that nice modest dwelling shall be the most famous in all London.' The bet was taken – in the course of four or five days Hook had written and despatched *one thousand* letters, conveying orders to tradesmen of every sort within the bills of mortality, all to be executed on one particular day, and as nearly as possible at one fixed hour. From waggons of coals and potatoes to books, prints, feathers, ices, jellies, and cranberry tarts – nothing in any way whatever available to any human being but was commanded from scores of rival dealers scattered over our 'pro-vince of bricks', from Wapping to Lambeth, from Whitechapel to Paddington. In 1809 Oxford Road was not approachable either from Westminster, or Mayfair, or from the City, otherwise than through a complicated series of lanes. It may be feebly and afar off guessed what the crash and jam and tumult of that day was. Hook had provided himself with a lodging nearly opposite the fated No.——; and there, with a couple of trusty allies, he watched the development of the midday melodrama. But some of the dramatis personæ were seldom if ever alluded to in later times.

He had no objection to bodying forth the arrival of the lord mayor and his chaplain, invited to take the deathbed confession of a peculating common councilman; but he would rather have buried in oblivion. that precisely the same liberty was taken with the Governor of the Bank, the chairman of the East India Company, a lord chief justice, a cabinet minister, — above all, with the Archbishop of Canterbury, and his Royal Highness the Commander-in-Chief. They all obeyed the summons — every pious and patriotic feeling had been most movingly appealed to; we are not sure that they all reached Berners Street: but the Duke of York's military punctuality and crimson liveries brought him to the point of attack before the poor widow's astonishment had risen to terror and despair. Perhaps no assassination, no conspiracy, no royal demise or ministerial revolution of recent times was a greater godsend to the newspapers than this audacious piece of mischief. In Hook's own theatrical world he was instantly suspected, but no sign escaped either him or his confidants. The affair was beyond that circle a serious one. Fierce were the growlings of the doctors and surgeons, scores of whom had been cheated of valuable hours. Attorneys, teachers of all kinds, male and female, hair-dressers, tailors, popular preachers, and parliamentary philanthropists, had been victimized in person, and were in their various notes vociferous. But the tangible material damage done was itself no joking matter. There had been an awful smashing of glass, china, harpsichords, and coach-panels. Many a horse had fallen never to rise again. Beer-barrels and wine-barrels had been overturned and exhausted with impunity amidst the press of countless multitudes. It had been a field-day for the pickpockets. There arose a fervent hue and cry for the detection of the wholesale deceiver and destroyer.

Mr. Theodore, we believe, found it convenient to

be laid up for a week or two by a severe fit of illness, and then promoted reconvalescence by a country tour.

The Quarterly Review, May 1843

William Beckford 1759–1844

William Beckford, the noted eccentric, was described variously by Disraeli as 'the man of the greatest taste' and by Fuseli as 'an actor but not a gentleman'. His life was a romantic *tour de force* shrouded in deep mystery. His funeral procession, the last spectacle of his own creation, was composed of his family and retainers dressed in costumes specially commissioned for the occasion, with an immense plume held high over the coffin. His body was placed in a costly granite sarcophagus made according to his instructions, and considerably sounder than the tower at Fonthill, one of his earlier creations.

The impatience of Mr. Beckford did not admit of the necessarily slow progress of a work of such dimensions as the Abbey of Fonthill, when constructed of solid materials. Timber and cement were therefore the principle articles in its composition, and every expedient was used to complete the building within a given time, regardless of the consequences that might almost have been expected to ensue. One immediate result of this injudicious haste was the destruction of the great tower which was carried up to the extreme height of 300 feet (and furnished with pinnacles and weather vanes), without time being allowed to complete its fastenings to the base on which it was erected. A gust of wind acting suddenly upon a large flag attached to a scaffold pole at its summit carried it off its base altogether. The fall was tremendous and sublime, and the only regret expressed by Mr. Beckford was that he had not witnessed the catastrophe.

The Annual Register of the year 1844

John Shirreff died 1844

Popular Edinburgh lunatic, who for a quarter of a century devoted his time to attending lectures at the University and frequenting the city's churches. His Sunday exhibitions were celebrated.

> Dressed with the most scrupulous care and cleanliness, in an antiquated costume of a semi-military character, with Hessian boots, he was to be seen every Sunday stalking through the streets at a rapid pace with his stick over his shoulder. His appearance was rendered still more grotesque by his wearing a deep green shade over his eyes with a pair of unusually large green spectacles poised near the extremity of his nose. He was sure to plant himself in the principal seat of the front gallery of one of the city churches, where he made himself still more conspicuous by standing up, sometimes sketching the portrait of the preacher while the rest of the congregation were composedly attending to the sermon. The High Church was his favourite resort for this purpose.

The Times, 23 August 1844

Funeral Directives

I've a great fancy to see my own funeral afore I die.
Castle Rackrent by Maria Edgeworth
(1767–1849)

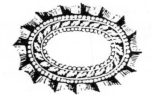

John Underwood *died* 1733

Conditions imposed on the beneficiaries of a will have ranged extensively from the practical and material to, more rarely, the intellectual.

Mr. John Underwood, of Whittlesea in Cambridgeshire. At his Burial, when the service was over, an Arch was turn'd over the coffin, in which was placed a small piece of white marble, with this inscription, *Non omnis moriar,* 1733. Then the 6 Gentlemen who followed him to the grave flung the last stanza of the 20th Ode of the 2nd Book of Horace. No bell was toll'd, no one invited but the 6 Gentlemen, and no relation follow'd his Corpse; the coffin was painted Green, and he laid in it with all his Cloaths on; under his Head was placed *Sanaden's Horace,* at his feet Bentley's *Milton;* in his Right Hand a small Greek Testament, in his Left Hand a little Edition of *Horace,* with this inscription, *Musis Amicus,* J. V., and Bentley's *Horace* under his Arse.

After the Ceremony was over they went back to his House, where his Sister had provided a cold supper; the cloth being taken away the Gentlemen sung the 31st Ode of the 1st Book of *Horace,* drank a chearful Glass, and went home about Eight. He left near 6000 l. to his Sister, on Condition of her observing this his will, order'd her to give each of the Gentlemen ten guineas, and desir'd they would not come in black Cloaths; the will ends thus—*Which done I would have them take a chearful Glass, and think no more of John Underwood.*

The Gentleman's Magazine, May 1733

76

John Frohock *died 1733*

John Frohock, Esq. of Ipswich, Counsellor at Law. Fearing he should be buried alive, he ordered his Coffin Lid to be made with Hinges, and 4 persons to attend his Corpse 8 days after Interment.

The Gentleman's Magazine, July 1733

Jeremiah Moore *1686–1753*

At his seat at Norton, near Stockton upon Tees, Durham, aged 57, Jeremiah Moore, Esq; He was the last of his family, and had, in the former part of his life, suffered extreme hardships through the cruelty of his eldest brother; by whose means he was carried into Turkish slavery, and at the time of his brother's death was a common seaman in the navy, having been pressed in the Mediterranean, after he had made his escape from the Turks. As he had experienced ill fortune, when he came to his estate, he converted it all into money and settled in the north, exercising acts of goodness to all his poor neighbours to whom he hath left largely. All the legatees are to receive their respective legacies on the 1st of March next, over a large bowl of punch, and they are yearly to commemorate that day as long as they live, it being the day on which he escaped from slavery.

The Scots Magazine, August 1753

William James *died* 1790

After a severe rub, Wm. James, assistant to the bowling-green at Solihull, Co. Warwick. The bearers of his corpse by the last particular request of the deceased, played a game of bowls upon the green, on their return from the funeral.

The Gentleman's Magazine, August 1790

Jean Baptista Muller *died* 1798

Once a dandy, always a dandy.

At Putney, Jean Baptista Muller, a native of Prussia. The singularity of his character may in some measure be collected from the following directions respecting his interment – 'I desire to be buried *within* the walls of the church, and interred in my buff embroidered waistcoat, my blue coat with a black collar, a pair of clean nankeen breeches, white silk stockings, my Prussian boots, my hair neatly dressed and powdered; and I particularly request, that my coffin may be made long enough to admit of my hussar cap being placed on my head. So dressed and accoutred, let me rest in peace.'

The Scots Magazine, March 1798

John Hare *died 1798*

John Hare, Esq. of Docking, in Norfolk, who left a written direction that after his decease his head should be severed from his body, and sewn on again.

Anti-Jacobin Review, June 1798

Stephen Girard *1750–1831*

Born in Bordeaux, Girard established himself as a merchant in Philadelphia shortly after the Declaration of Independence. He founded the Bank of Stephen Girard and was one of the original directors of the Second United States Bank. Enterprising and philanthropic, 'To rest is to rust' was a favourite saying of his, and Girard College is a monument to his munificence. He bequeathed two million dollars to endow the College, making, it was reported, one notable stipulation in his will:

> I enjoin and require that no ecclesiastic, missionary, or minister of any sect whatsoever, shall ever hold or exercise any station or duty whatever in the said College; nor shall any such person ever be admitted for any purpose, or as a visitor, within the premises appropriated to the purposes of the said College.

The Gentleman's Magazine, March 1832

Gardeners and
Naturalists

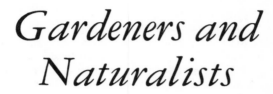

Here at the fountain's sliding foot,
Or at some fruit-tree's mossy root,
Casting the body's vest aside,
My soul into the boughs does glide;
There, like a bird, it sits, and sings,
Then whets and combs its silver wings;
And, till prepar'd for longer flight,
Waves in its plumes the various light.

The Garden by Andrew Marvell
(1621–1678)

Comte de Buffon 1707–1788

The prolific French writer and naturalist, of whom the Editor of the *Mercure* wrote: 'France has been unluckily deprived, within this century, of many writers of real genius and the brilliant shoots of the learned age of Louis XIV, but the greatest loss this kingdom ever suffered is certainly the Count de Buffon's death.' The presence of 20,000 spectators crowding the streets through which the Count's hearse passed and showing as much interest as if the ceremony were for a monarch, is evidence of an age in which intellect was regarded as highly as birth. The Count's literary style was often theatrical and turgid, a style which is strongly reflected whether consciously or unconsciously in the following lines, written by a fellow countryman.

Four bright lamps are now totally extinguished in France. They were suspended in the Temple of Genius; and from the bosom of this kingdom diffused their extensive light all over the universe. One, after having dissipated the clouds that enveloped the causes of the grandeur and decline of the Roman empire, threw a new and splendid light over the immense volumes of law; with the great Montesquieu this lamp went out. Brilliant and beneficent rays, with due gradations of heat, like the solar ones, issued from the second lamp, which gave new charms to the Sciences, and explained them in a clear and seducing manner: the Arts found, in this effulgent light, an amiable and sure guide: History was taught a quick, steady, and lively march: Poetry all the *eclat* and splendour of the celestial mansions whence she springs: Philosophy appeared clad in the soft attirement of the Graces; and Man felt in his heart stronger emotions of humanity: Voltaire's death extinguished this wonderful lamp. A flame, now devouring like those of the Tropics, now soft as the genial rays of blushing Morn; now melancholy, tender, and affecting as the fair beams of the Cynthian Goddess, inflamed the enraptured soul with the holy enthusiasm of Virtue, and cast over Morality the attracting colours of Voluptuousness. The country smiled with such bewitching charms, that man longed to partake of rural toils and sports. At the appearance of this powerful flame, soon vanished barbarous Prejudice, the origin of Bondage and of Tyranny. The unnatural shackles that confined children were broken with the chains that enthralled the mind; Heaven, and the august countenance of the Almighty, stood then confessed before astonished man, who became good, humane, and happy in the charming visions of Hope. With Rousseau's breath the fostering flame abated; but a new star, by Nature formed to spread a wonderous light over all her works, began to shine with a majestic and unparalleled lustre. Its course was marked by Pomp, its motion by Harmony, its repose by Serenity. All eyes, even the weakest, were fond of contemplating it. From its refulgent car it spread magnificence over the universe; and as God assembled, in the narrow space of the ark, all the works of the creation, so this great luminary re-united on the verdant banks of the Seine, the animals, the vegetables, and the minerals, that are dispersed in the four quarters of the world. All forms, all colours, all riches, and all instincts, were offered to our eyes, and our intellectual faculties. All things were developed, all things were ennobled, and adorned with splendour, interest, or grace. But a sable funeral veil is spread, alas! over this bright and wonderful star. Nature silently mourns her loss. With Buffon's life ended the fourth lamp; and nothing now remains for his surviving admirers but the sentiment of their loss, and the despair of repairing it.

Journal de Paris, 1788

Sir Henry Liddell 1749–1791

Non-native species have in the past been introduced into England for fairly unorthodox reasons, as evidenced by this journey to Lapland which was made in 1786.

> At Bath, Sir Henry George Ravensworth Liddell, bart, of Durham. He possessed an immense estate in the North, where he was distinguished for a warm and generous spirit, which sometimes, however, carried him into romantic transactions. His excursion to Lapland upon a wager, and his return with two Lapland girls and rein-deer are well remembered. The Lapland girls were returned safe to their native country, after an absence of several months, with £50 and a cargo of trinkets; and the rein-deer have bred in England.
>
> *The Gentleman's Magazine,* December 1791

Humphry Repton 1752–1818

English landscape gardener, who ceased to practise in 1811 when he was maimed in an accident returning with his daughters from a ball.

> Mr. Repton both lived and died in *character*. His mind and time had been uniformly occupied with his professional pursuits during a long series of years; and he concluded his life and labours, with a quotation from the works of a celebrated foreigner, who possessed congenial taste and feelings with himself: 'Allons mes amis, il faut cultiver nos Jardins!'
>
> *The Annual Biography and Obituary for the year 1819*

Charles Waterton *1782–1865*

The renowned naturalist, traveller and eccentric, Charles Waterton, was a friend of many, including the author W. M. Thackeray, who refers to him in *The Newcomers* as 'a good man. I know that his works are made to square with his faith, that he dines on a crust, lives as chastely as a hermit, and gives his all to the poor'. Long before he died, he erected his own mausoleum and and left detailed instructions for his funeral, requesting that his body be carried by boat over his lake to the mausoleum and the mourners follow in its wake.

Charles Waterton, esq., of Walton Hall in the County of York, the celebrated naturalist and traveller, died on the 27th ult. at his seat, Walton Hall, near Wakefield. *The Wanderings,* now a standard work, created on its first publication a furore, and, particularly the author's account of his ride on a cayman or crocodile's back. He was the first bird-stuffer in the world, and his collections in that way at Walton are magnificent. Charles Waterton, with all his many eccentricities – written, spoken and enacted – was of a truly gentle spirit. He was benevolent to all – benevolent, it may literally be said, to man and brute. One of the squire's well known traits was never to allow a shot to be fired on his grounds except to keep down the rabbits, whose impudent invasions were too much even for him. The result was that in Walton Park many a rare bird and animal has made its haunt in safety, and the curious circumstances may be therein seen of herons and other equally shy members of the feathered tribe remaining unmoved at the report of a gun. He liberally threw open the Park, and it was the resort, during the summer months, of numerous pleasure-parties.

The Illustrated London News, 3 June 1865

Sir Joseph Paxton 1801–1865

'England is the nursing mother of self-made men, and in this generation the number of them has been greater than in any former age',
declared *The Times*. Paxton, who came of humble origins, had the
good fortune to attract the notice of the Duke of Devonshire. As
gardener at Chatsworth he 'set the example of that princely development of grounds and pleasances which now marks the country homes
of the great English families'. He planned the hothouses, where the
great water-lily, *Victoria regia,* was first compelled to blossom, and the
grand conservatory, the precursor of the Crystal Palace. Covering
nearly an acre of ground, this had 'an underground railway for the use
of the gardeners and workmen, an elaborate and successful system of
heating and ventilation, and an ingenious ridge-and-furrow arrange-
ment of the glass for the double purpose of increasing its power of
resisting hail-storms and facilitating the rapid passage of rainwater'.

It was as a gardener that Paxton first made a name for
himself; but it was in the large sense of the word, as
one who by a kind of instinct had the beautiful in
nature at command to embellish the landscape, and,
without the ordinary process of scientific study, had
practically all the laws of plant life at his call. In these
delightful pursuits a vigorous, kindly, and sensitive
disposition expanded congenially. He had many
friends, but they belonged to no set, or party, or
clique; nor was there anything narrow or sectarian
about the man in his relations with other men.
Friendship was a plant which he loved to cultivate
wherever it would grow.

The Ilustrated London News, 17 June 1865

Charles Darwin 1809–1882

'To attempt to reckon up the influence which Mr. Darwin's multifarious work has had upon modern thought and modern life in all its phases seems as difficult a task as it would be to count the number and trace the extent of the sound-waves from a park of artillery', declared *The Times*. 'Through his influence the whole method of seeking after knowledge has been changed, and the increasing rapidity with which the results are every day developed becomes more and more bewildering. To what remote corners in religion, in legislation, in education, in everyday life, from Imperial Assemblies and venerable Universities to humble board schools and remote Scottish manses, the impetus initiated on board the "Beagle" and developed at the quiet and comfortable home at Beckenham has reached, those who are in the whirl and sweep of it are not in a position to say.'

Animal and vegetable life as it is lived was his lifelong study. He allowed nature to work in its own way, superintending the process. In the words of *The Saturday Review* obituary: 'He did not take life at any one point and describe what he saw, but let life go on and described the stages of existence. In order to see how worms change the surface of the earth, he watched the ways of worms for forty years. He was always doing something with his worms – weighing their secretions, trying how they liked a candle or a piano.'

'To make experiments by watching the minute processes of life year after year demands leisure, means absence of interruption and freedom from anxiety', and in this Darwin was fortunate:

> The shelter of a college, the modest pomp of a Prussian court, or a well-ordered country home in England, may equally give the man of scientific genius the two things he needs, time and peace. But in its own way the life of Mr. Darwin was an ideal life. He commanded in youth such advantages of a mixed education as the training of a public school, of the University of Edinburgh, and of Cambridge could give him. He had never to face the problem which so often crushes ability, if it seldom represses genius, how to live while learning. Mr. Darwin

could wait and work, could think or travel, free from the presence of pecuniary anxiety. When the great opportunity of his life fell in his way, and he was allowed to join the *Beagle* expedition, the ardour with which he volunteered to fill the post of travelling naturalist was not chilled by the thought that he might be ruining his prospects in life. During the five years which the expedition occupied, Mr. Darwin suffered from almost constant sea-sickness, and his constitution was so shaken by his sufferings that during the rest of his long life he could only preserve a delicate health by unremitting care. But the quiet and seclusion to which he was condemned not only fell in with his tastes, but permitted him to pursue his special studies without a pause and without distraction. Happy in his fortune and happy in his marriage, he also had the unusual happiness of finding among his own children the best and most zealous of coadjutors. Under these conditions a sweet and gentle nature blossomed into perfection. Arrogance, irritability, and envy, the faults that ordinarily beset men of genius, were not so much conquered as non-existent in a singularly simple and generous mind. It never occurred to him that it would be to his gain to show that he and not someone else was the author of a discovery. If he was appealed to for help by a fellow-worker, the thought never passed into his mind that he had secrets to divulge which would lessen his importance. It was science, not the fame of science, that he loved, and he helped science by the temper in which he approached it. He had to say things that were distasteful to a large portion of the public; but he won the ear even of his most adverse critics by his manifest absence of a mere desire to shine, by his modesty, and by his courtesy. He told honestly what he thought to be the truth, but he told it without a wish to triumph or to wound. There is an arrogance of unorthodoxy as well as an arrogance of orthodoxy, and if ideas that a quarter of a century ago were regarded with dread are now accepted without a pang, the rapidity of the change of opinion, if not the change itself, is largely due to the fact that the leading exponent of these ideas was the least arrogant of men.

The Saturday Review, 22 April 1882

Lawyers and Merchants

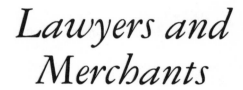

For so work the honey-bees,
Creatures that by a rule in nature teach
The act of order to a peopled kingdom.
They have a king and officers of sorts;
Where some, like magistrates, correct at home,
Others, like merchants, venture trade abroad . . .

Henry V by William Shakespeare
(1564–1616)

Mr Philips *1624–1742*

Strict discipline has always had its adherents, even on the wrong side of the law.

> Mr. Philips of Thorner, near Leeds, in Yorkshire, aged 118. Being Constable about 90 years ago, he upon some Disorders, committed two of Oliver Cromwell's soldiers in the town-stocks, who, far from resenting it, wish'd that every one of his men had but half his courage.

> *The Gentleman's Magazine*, January 1742

Richard Nash *(Beau Nash) 1674–1762*

After a period in the army, where he dressed the part, according to Goldsmith, 'to the very edge of his finances', Beau Nash reverted to law since he found that 'the profession of arms required attendance and duty, and often encroached upon those hours he could have wished to dedicate to softer purposes'. From the age of thirty, he was universally regarded as the uncrowned king of Bath, renowned for his whimsical dress and behaviour.

> Richard Nash, Esq., or as he is commonly called, Beau Nash, was born in the town of Swanley, in Glamorganshire, on the 18th of October, 1674. Educated at Caermarthen School and from thence sent to Jesus College in Oxford, Mr. Nash thereby distinguished himelf not by application to study, but by assiduity in intrigue.

Mr. Nash having quitted College, bought himself a pair of colours, and entered into the army; but still continuing his intrigues and finding that the profits of his commission would not enable him to support his expenses, he exchanged the military life for the study of the law, and accordingly entered his name in the Temple books.

Though Nash acquired no riches by his office, he gained many friends. With these he conversed with the greatest familiarity, and his generosity and benevolence already began to shew themselves amidst all his poverty. An instance of this kind is told us about this time which does him no small honour. When he was to give in his accounts to the Master of the Temple, among other articles, he charged, 'For making one man happy £10.' Being questioned about the meaning of so strange an item, he frankly declared that happening to overhear a poor man tell his wife and a large family of children that £10 would make him happy, he could not avoid trying the experiment, adding, that if they did not choose to acquiesce in his charge, he was ready to refund the money. The master, struck with such an uncommon instance of good nature, publicly thanked him and desired that the sum might be doubled, as a proof of their satisfaction.

On the other hand we are told, that while the poor blessed his charity and munificence, his creditors complained with great reason of his injustice; and amongst other stories related of him to this purpose, is one which informs us of a friend's not being able to procure a just debt of him but by the employing of another person to borrow a sum off Nash to the amount. The person obeyed, and readily obtained that from Nash's generosity which the other had often implored in vain from his justice.

The Annual Register of the year 1762

William Evans *died 1795*

In the county of Anglesey, in his 75th year, Mr. Wm. Evans, who was upwards of 40 years the chief clerk in the prothonotary's office for the counties of Anglesey, Carnarvon, and Merioneth; and well known to all the counsel and practitioners for his eccentricity of character. He had been spending the evening previous to his death among a few companions, one of whom is said to have had recourse to that mistaken joke, that bastard species of wit, an infusion of jalap in the beverage, which operated so powerfully on the constitution of poor Evans, that he literally died of a diarrhoea. – Among other peculiaries, he was a sort of epicure in wigs and walking-sticks; and for many years past had been so laborious in enlarging both his wiggery and stickery, that he has left a competent number for the heads and hands of all the ancient gentlemen of taste in the principality. In the early part of his life he felt a tender passion for three amiable fair-ones; and, as an abundant proof of the warmth of his attachment, even till death, he has, amongst other curious bequests, left to each of these virgin pullets both wisdom and support, namely, a wig and a walking-stick.

The Gentleman's Magazine, April 1795

Richard Moon 1763–1800

An attorney at law from Coln, Co. Lancaster, a gentle and much-loved man, Richard Moon was accorded at his funeral an old-fashioned mark of respect.

In the North of England a custom is still retained from our Catholic ancestors; placing lights in the windows, as the corpse of a dear and beloved object passes to its long home. In the evening, on the road from Manchester to Coln, whilst every eye, not only of the numerous gentry that attended, but even of the common gazers in the street, was steeped in tears, the large and splendid lights in Burnley testified the regard of the town for this amiable young man. Thence the cottage windows of the two townships of Marsden beamed with fainter lights, till the funereal splendour again commenced in the town of Coln. And where those, who heaved the passing tribute of a sign, could not afford the lustre of a candle, the weaver's lamps, placed in the windows, supplied its place. In one instance, where the poor cottager could perhaps supply neither candle nor lamp, and yet could not refuse some frail memorial of his gratitude and mournful regard, he stood at his door with two large splinters of deal wood lighted upon the occasion.

The Gentleman's Magazine, Supplement to 1800

Sir Francis Baring 1726–1810

At Lee, Kent, aged 74, Sir Francis Baring, bart, one of the Directors of the East India Company, and formerly M.P. for Taunton. His talents were of a very superior cast and highly improved by reading. Few men understood the real interests of trade better; and it may surely be added, few men ever arrived at the highest rank and honour of commercial life with more unsullied integrity. At his death, he was unquestionably the first merchant in Europe; first in knowledge and talents, and first in character and opulence. His name was known and respected in every commercial quarter of the globe; and by the East India Company, and other public trading bodies, he was consulted as a man of consummate knowledge and inflexible honour.

His private, as well as public life, if faithfully delineated, would form a most instructive lesson to the mercantile world; and a lesson particularly necessary at a time when so many seem to forget or despise the genuine attributes of an English merchant, and aspire at sudden and unsubstantial wealth and credit, by the paltry speculation of mere fraud and low cunning.

The Gentleman's Magazine, September 1810

T. Gordon *died 1810*

At Spittal, near Berwick, after a life of strange vicissitudes and wonderful escapes, aged above 90, T. Gordon. It is related of him, that at one period of his life, being under sentence of death in Edinburgh gaol, one of the county magistrates, speaking warmly about the prisoner, said that 'all the Gordons should be hanged.' This speech was conveyed to the then Duchess of Gordon, who, feeling for the honour of the name, immediately exerted all her influence in behalf of Gordon, and succeeded in getting his sentence changed to a few years' solitary confinement.

The Gentleman's Magazine, November 1810

Lord Erskine *1750–1823*

Called to the Bar in 1778, Thomas Erskine achieved immediate success with his brilliant defence of Captain Baillie, lieutenant-governor of Greenwich Hospital, threatened with a criminal prosecution for libel. He was elected Member of Parliament for Portsmouth and in 1802 was appointed Chancellor to the Prince of Wales, but it was as an advocate, of 'unremitting diligence, most laborious habits of investigation, and unimpeachable integrity', that he shone. To his intellectual qualifications were added the no less useful advantages of person, countenance and voice. 'His features were good, and capable of infinite variety of expression; the whole animated and intelligent at all times, and occasionally lighted up and beaming with a sweetness which we never saw in equal perfection in any other human face. His manner set off the whole. The clear melodious tones of his voice were nicely, and almost scientifically, modulated to the subject in hand, and accompanied by action most inimitably graceful; such as those who have not seen it, can form no notion of from the stiff attitudes and boisterous gestures of the degenerate Performers of the present day.'

He not only made himself from his brief a perfect master of his Client's case, but he brought to his service the full measure of his zealous feeling, and the perfect exercise of his brilliant talents. He condescended even to have recourse to little artifices, pardonable in themselves, to aid the illusion. He examined the Court the night before the trial, in order to select the most advantageous place for addressing the Jury, and when the cause was called on, the Court and audience were usually kept waiting in anxious suspense a few minutes before the celebrated stranger made his appearance, and when at length he gratified their impatience, a particularly nice wig, and a pair of new yellow gloves distinguished and embellished his person beyond the more ordinary costume of the Barristers of the Circuit.

The Gentleman's Magazine, December 1823

Jeremy Bentham 1748–1832

Philosopher and writer on jurisprudence and ethics, Jeremy Bentham was a persistent and influential critic of British political and judicial institutions. His early manner of writing was clear and concise but it became increasingly diffuse towards the end of his life. In *The Examiner* in 1832 it was remarked that 'Felicity of expression abounds even in those of his works which are generally unreadable.' Another obituary notice included the comment:

> As a writer Bentham was very obscure; but he had able friends, who made some of his numerous works intelligible, and who helped him to that fame which even his own obscurities could not strangle.

The Gentleman's Magazine, July 1832

Howqua died 1844

Senior Hong Kong merchant of notorious wealth and success.

> The Chinese Government had the greatest confidence in Howqua, who, to the last, retained an inveterate aversion to new customs and modern fashions, whilst he clung with the most conservative tenacity to the old corrupt system by which his vast wealth was mainly accumulated.
>
> *The Times*, 9 January 1844

99

Sir George Rose 1782–1873

A lawyer by profession, Rose first achieved a reputation as a wit with the following epitome of the arguments and ruling in a certain case in court:

> *Mr. Leach made a speech,*
> *Angry, neat, and long;*
> *Mr. Hart, on the other part,*
> *Was right, but dull and long.*
> *Mr. Parker made that darker*
> *Which was dark enough without;*
> *Mr. Cook quoted his book,*
> *And the Chancellor said 'I doubt'.*

He specialized, however, in puns – described by Boswell as 'among the smaller excellences of lively conversation' – and several examples were given in a memoir of him.

Dining on one occasion with the late Lord Langdale, his host was speaking of the very diminutive church in Langdale, of which his lordship was patron. 'It is not bigger,' said Lord Langdale, 'than this dining-room.' 'No,' returned Sir George, *'and the living not half so good.'*

A friend who had been appointed to a judgeship in one of the colonies, was long after describing to Rose the agonies he had suffered on the voyage out from sea-sickness. Sir George listened with much interest to the recital of his friend's sufferings, and then said, in a tone of deep commiseration, 'It's a mercy you did not throw up your appointment.'

Macmillan's Magazine, February 1874

Sir George Jessel 1824–1883

Master of the Rolls, renowned for his rapid, satisfactory and punctual discharge of legal business.

> When he had fairly laid out his estate in Kent, it became his favourite amusement in the holidays to spend his days there in harmless rural pleasures. He did not shoot or hunt, but would collect and classify fungi, or would throw into the marking out of the tennis-lawn the same close attention to the matter in hand which was invaluable to him in deciding cases.

The Times, 22 March 1883

Sir Joseph Whitworth 1803–1887

The career of Sir Joseph Whitworth showed what possibilities of achievement lay within reach of any lad in Victorian Britain who cultivated assiduously his opportunities and had the genius and self-restraint indispensable for success. At the age of fourteen he began work in a Derbyshire cotton mill. In 1833, at the age of thirty, he had set up his own business in Manchester as a manufacturer of engineers' tools, having discovered a way of producing an absolutely plane surface of metal and devised the standardization of screw threads. At the Great Exhibition in 1851 he appeared as the maker of the true plane and a measuring machine that was accurate to a millionth of an inch. The importance of his inventions and methods of orderly production is illustrated in the following excerpt from his obituary.

> The Crimean War began, and Sir Charles Napier demanded of the Admiralty 120 gunboats, each with engines of 60 horse-power, for the campaign of 1855 in the Baltic. There were just ninety days in which to meet this requisition, and, short as the time was, the building of the gunboats presented no difficulty. It was otherwise, however, with the engines, and the Admiralty were in despair. Suddenly, by a flash of the mechanical genius which was inherent in him, the

101

late Mr. John Penn solved the difficulty, and solved it quite easily. He had a pair of engines on hand of the exact size. He took them to pieces and he distributed the parts among the best machine shops in the country, telling each to make ninety sets exactly in all respects to sample. The orders were executed with unfailing regularity, and he actually completed ninety sets of engines of 60 horse-power in ninety-days — a feat which made the great Continental Powers stare with wonder, and which was possible only because the Whitworth standards of measurement and of accuracy and finish were by that time thoroughly recognised and established throughout the country.

The Times, 24 January 1887

Lord Coleridge *1820–1894*

John Duke Coleridge, famed as a barrister on the Western Circuit for his 'silver-tongued' eloquence, was appointed Solicitor-General in 1868 and Attorney-General in 1871. Among the famous cases with which he was involved was the trial of the Tichborne Claimant. His cross-examination of the Claimant lasted for twenty-one days and he made in his reply the longest speech that had been heard in a court of law. He became Lord Chief Justice in 1880.

No recollections of the Lord Chief Justice would be complete without mentioning his brilliancy and the extent and variety of his resources as a conversationalist. He had known most of the celebrated men of his time. With many he was linked by ties of close friendship, and his retentive memory poured out a flood of stories, legal, ecclesiastical, and academic, about men, books, and affairs for full half a century. An American visitor to Ottery with a turn for statistics computed that in the course of three rainy days the Chief Justice told 200 stories, most of them good, and all intended to cheer an Ambassador, also a guest, who had caught a chill. *The Times,* 15 June 1894

Literati

Jane went to Paradise:
That was only fair,
Good Sir Walter met her first,
And led her up the stair.
Henry and Tobias,
And Miguel of Spain,
Stood with Shakespeare at the top
To welcome Jane.

Jane's Marriage by Rudyard Kipling
(1865–1936)

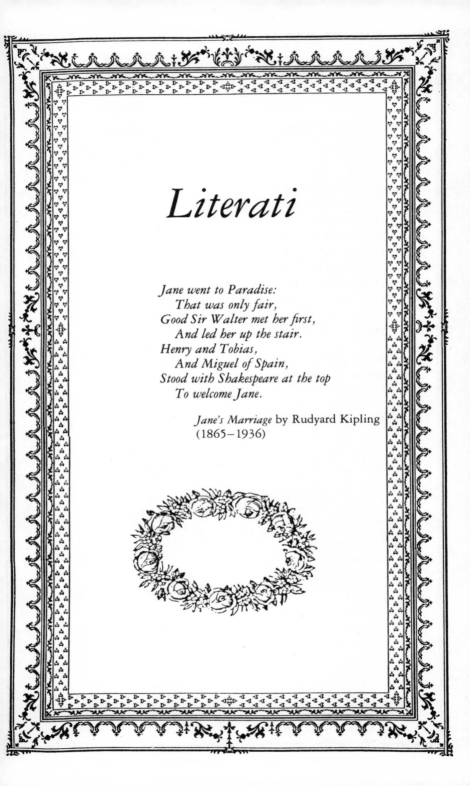

Esther Johnson died 1728

Although it is not known for certain whether Dean Swift ever married Esther Johnson, or 'Stella' as she is usually known, he clearly loved her. One of the mementos of their relationship is an envelope containing a lock of her hair. The news of her death reached him one Sunday evening in January 1728.

> A servant brought me a note, with an account of the truest, most virtuous and valuable friend, that I or perhaps any other person was ever blessed with.
>
> I knew her from six years old, and had some share in her education, by directing what books she should read, and perpetually instructing her in the principles of honour and virtue: from which she never swerved in any one action or moment of her life.

The Death of Mrs. Johnson from the last two posthumous volumes of Dean Swift's works.

Jonathan Swift 1667–1745

Swift's insight was as keen as it was one-sided, and his hatred of vice seemed always to be underlined by a recognition of the futility in this world of virtue or wisdom or sanity – hence his bequests foreshadowed in his own *Verses on His Own Death* (1731)

> *He gave the little wealth he had,*
> *To build a House for Fools and Mad;*
> *And shew'd by one satyric Touch,*
> *No Nation wanted it so much:*

At Dublin, aged 78, Dr. Jonathan Swift, Dean of St. Patrick's, Dublin; whose genius, works, learning, and charity, are universally admired. He bequeathed the bulk of his estate, which is about 12,000 l. to build and endow an hospital for lunaticks, idiots, and incurables, which is to be called St. Patrick's and to be erected near Stevens's.

The Scots Magazine, October 1745

Oliver Goldsmith *1731–1774*

Goldsmith, the Anglo-Irish author best known for *The Vicar of Wakefield*, was regarded by many of his contemporaries as 'vain, acutely sensitive to neglect and hostile to criticism'. The writer of the following, however, who had 'lived with him upon the most friendly footing for a great number of years, and who never felt any sorrow more sensibly than that which was occasioned by his death' was determined to put the record straight.

A feature in his character we cannot help laying before the reader. Previous to the publication of his *Deserted Village*, the book-seller had given him a note for one hundred guineas for the copy, which the Doctor mentioned, a few hours after, to one of his friends, who observed, it was a very great sum for so short a performance. 'In truth,' replied Goldsmith, 'I think so too; I have not been easy since I received it; therefore, I will go back, and return him his note;' which he absolutely did, and left it entirely to the book-seller to pay him according to the profits produced by the sale of the piece, which turned out very considerable.

During the last rehearsal of his comedy, entitled, *She Stoops to Conquer*, which Mr. Colman had no opinion would succeed, on the Doctor's objecting to the repetition of one of Tony Lumpkin's speeches, being apprehensive it might injure the play, the manager with great keenness replied, 'Psha, my dear Doctor, do not be fearful of squibs, when we have been sitting almost these two hours upon a barrel of gun-powder.' The piece, however, contrary to Mr. Colman's expectation, was received with uncommon applause by the audience; and Goldsmith's pride was so hurt by the severity of the above observation, that it entirely put an end to his friendship for the gentleman that made it.

Notwithstanding the great success of his pieces, by some of which it is asserted, upon good authority, he cleared 1800 l. in one year, his circumstances were by no means in a prosperous situation; which was partly owing to the liberality of his disposition, and partly to an unfortunate habit he had contracted of gaming, the arts of which he knew very little of, and, consequently became the prey of those who were unprincipled enough to take advantage of his simplicity.

The learned leisure he loved to enjoy was too often interrupted by distresses which arose from the liberality of his temper, and which sometimes threw him into loud fits of passion; but this impetuosity was corrected upon a moment's reflection, and his servants have been known, upon these occasions, purposely to throw themselves in his way, that they might profit by it immediately after; for he who had the good fortune to be reproved was certain of being rewarded for it. The universal esteem in which his poems were held, and the repeated pleasure they give in the perusal, is a striking test of their merit. He was a studious and correct observer of nature, happy in the selection of his images, in the choice of his subjects, and in the harmony of his versification; and, though his embarrassed situation prevented him from putting the last hand to many of his productions, his *Hermit,* his *Traveller,* and his *Deserted Village,* bid fair to claim a place among the most finished pieces in the English language.

The Annual Register of the year 1774

Samuel Johnson 1709–1784

When Dr Johnson took Boswell with him on his tour to the Hebrides in 1773, Boswell's wife remarked that though she had seen 'many a bear led by a man she had never before seen a man led by a bear'. His father did not take kindly either to his son's 'going over Scotland with a brute'. Boswell's feelings for the noted lexicographer and character were, however, very different, as demonstrated by the following piece that he wrote after Johnson's death.

Dr. Samuel Johnson's character, religious, moral, political, and literary, nay, his figure and manner, are, I believe, more generally known than those of almost any man; yet it may not be superfluous here to attempt a sketch of him. Let my readers then remember that he was a sincere and zealous christian, of the high church of England and monarchical principles, which he would not tamely suffer to be questioned; steady and inflexible in maintaining the obligations of piety and virtue, both from a regard to the order of society, and from a veneration for the Great Source of all order: correct, nay stern in his taste; hard to please, and easily offended; impetuous and irritable in his temper, but of a most humane and benevolent heart; having a mind stored with a vast and various collection of learning and knowledge, which he communicated with peculiar perspicuity, and force, in rich and choice expression. He united a most logical head with a most fertile imagination, which gave him an extraordinary advantage in arguing; for he could reason close or wide, as he saw best for the moment. He could, when he chose it, be the greatest sophist that ever wielded a weapon in the schools of declamation; but he indulged this only in conversation; for he owned he sometimes talked for victory: he was too conscientious to make errour permanent and pernicious by deliberately writing it. He was conscious of his superiority. He loved praise when it was brought to him; but he was too proud to seek for it. He was somewhat susceptible of flattery. His mind was so full of imagery, that he might have been perpetually a poet. It has been often remarked, that in his poetical pieces, which it is to be regretted are so few, because so excellent, his style is easier than in his prose. There is deception in this: it is not easier, but better suited to the dignity of verse; as one may dance with grace, whose motions, in ordinary walking, – in the common step, are awkward. He had a constitutional melancholy, the clouds of which darkened the brightness of his fancy, and gave a gloomy cast to his whole course of thinking: yet, though grave and awful in his deportment, when he thought it necessary or proper, – he frequently indulged himself in pleasantry and sportive sallies. He was prone to superstition, but not to credulity. Though his imagination might incline him to a belief of the marvellous, and the mysterious, his vigorous reason examined the evidence with jealousy. He had a loud voice, and a flow of deliberate utterance, which no doubt gave some additional weight to the sterling metal of his conversation. Lord Pembroke said once to me at Wilton, with a happy pleasantry and some truth, that 'Dr. Johnson's sayings would not appear so extraordinary, were it not for his bow-wow way.' But I admit the truth of this only on some occasions; the Messiah, played upon the Canterbury organ, is more sublime than when played upon an inferior instrument: but very slight music will seem grand, when conveyed to the ear through that majestic medium. While therefore Doctor Johnson's sayings are read, let his manner be taken along with them. Let it however be observed that the sayings are generally great; that, though he might be an ordinary composer at times, he was for the most part a Handel. – His person was large, robust, I may say approaching to the gigantick, and grown unwieldy from corpulency. His countenance was naturally of the cast of an ancient statue, but somewhat disfigured by the scars of that evil, which, it was formerly imagined the royal touch could cure. He was now in his sixty-fourth year, and was become a little dull of hearing. His sight had always been somewhat weak; yet so much does mind govern and even supply the deficiency of organs, that his perceptions were uncommonly quick and accurate. His head, and sometimes also his body, shook with a kind of motion like the effect of a palsy: he appeared to be frequently disturbed by cramps, or convulsive contractions, of the nature of that distemper called St. Vitus's dance. He wore a full suit of plain brown cloaths, with twisted hair buttons of the same colour, a large bushy greyish wig, a plain shirt, black worsted stockings, and silver buckles. Upon this tour, when journeying, he wore boots, and a very wide brown cloth great coat, with pockets which might have almost held the two volumes of his folio dictionary; and he carried in his hand a large English oak stick. Let me not be censured for mentioning such minute particulars. Every thing relative to so great a man is worth observing. I remember Dr. Adam Smith, in his rhetorical lectures at Glasgow, told us he was glad to know that Milton wore latchets in his shoes, instead of buckles.

James Boswell, *Journal of a Tour to the Hebrides* (1785)

Monsieur Savary *died 1788*

Critics should remember that an author's pride is at best, delicate; at worst, fatal.

Lately, of a disorder incident to sedentary persons, an obstruction in his liver, M. Savary, author of *Les Voyages d'Egypte*. He was preparing a Dictionary and Grammar of the Arabian language. The severe remarks of other writers, and particularly Volney's, on his travels, had not a little ruffled his mind and very likely accelerated his death. He was hardly forty years old.

The Scots Magazine, March 1788

Job Maurice 1695–1793

Mr Maurice was fortunate, it seems, to die of natural causes in America.

In New Hampshire in America, aged 98, Mr. Job Maurice; who had written very ingeniously on the distresses of the first adventurers in the American regions, when the Spaniards literally ate the natives, and Frenchmen devoured one another; when Englishmen, who had been there, were afterwards shown in London as skeletons.

The Gentleman's Magazine, July 1793

Eliza Berkeley 1734–1800

Writer with a strong propensity for satire. Her thoughts, words and actions were influenced by her religious fervour but this 'did not *always* preserve her from inveterate anger and severe invectives, inconsistent with the essence of Christianity and the mild precepts of that Gospel she adored'.

> In conversation, as in writing, she was extremely entertaining, except to those who wished also to entertain, when she appeared too redundant in her stories and anecdotes.
>
> *The Gentleman's Magazine*, November 1800

Robert Bloomfield 1766–1823

Poetical shoemaker, author of *Farmer's Boy* which was composed in a garret and achieved a remarkable success: it was estimated that twenty-six thousand copies of the poem were sold within three years of its publication in 1800. He died half blind and in wretched poverty.

> There are a numerous host of fabricators of verse, who may be compared to milliners and tailors, who do not concern themselves about the *quality* of the figure which they are employed to clothe; but think all merit lies in the *dress* which they furnish for them; and who of course take both the materials and forms of their ornaments from the last favourite fashions of the market. Bloomfield's care was directed to the choice of the figure to be dressed; and then he put it forth in the simplest habiliments of mere necessity, through which its native beauty might shine unencumbered.
>
> *The Gentleman's Magazine*, December 1823

Lieutenant-Colonel John Macdonald *died 1831*

John Macdonald, son of Flora Macdonald, the Scottish Jacobite heroine, 'who so materially assisted Prince Charles in evading the English soldiery in 1746', paid the following tribute, which was quoted in his obituary, to the influence of Sir Walter Scott's books:

'I well recollect,' remarked the late Colonel, when speaking of the results of Sir Walter Scott's writings, 'my arrival in London, about half a century ago, on my way to India; and the disapprobation expressed in the streets of my Tartan dress; but now I see with satisfaction the variegated Highland manufacture prevalent, as a favourite and tasteful costume, from the humble cottage to the superb castle. To Sir Walter Scott's elegant and fascinating writings we are to ascribe this wonderful revolution in public sentiment.'

The Gentleman's Magazine, January 1832

Sir Walter Scott 1771–1832

The Gentleman's Magazine devoted twenty-three pages to a memoir of Sir Walter Scott when he died. The account of one who 'shone equally as a good and virtuous man, as he did in his capacity as the first fictitious writer of the age' begins with his childhood and upbringing in the Scottish Borders and the composition of a war-song for the Royal Mid-Lothian Cavalry, of which he was adjutant. It describes his early versifications and the 'raids' he made into Liddesdale to collect specimens of the popular poetry of the district, visiting many of the places alluded to in the ballads and legends. As recorded by a friend, he had a singular, even mysterious, manner of committing them to memory.

> According to Mr. Shortreed's distinct recollection, he used neither pencil nor pen, but, seizing upon any twig or piece of wood which he could find, marked it by means of a clasp-knife, with various notches, which his companion believed to represent particular ideas in his own mind; and these Mr. Shortreed afterwards found strung up before him in his study at home, like the *nick sticks* over a baker's desk, or the string alphabet of a blind man. When his own pockets were inconveniently stuffed with these notes, he would request Mr. Shortreed to take charge of a few; and often that gentleman has discharged as much timber from his various integuments, as, to use his own phrase, quoted from Burns, 'might have mended a mill'.
>
> *The Gentleman's Magazine*, October 1832

Maria Edgeworth 1767–1849

An Irish novelist possibly best known for her novel *Castle Rackrent*, Maria Edgeworth's early attempts at fiction were somewhat melodramatic relating, for example, how one of her heroes wore a mask made of the dried skin taken from a dead man's face. Her influence on Sir Walter Scott was considerable. In the general preface of the 1829 edition to his novels Sir Walter Scott wrote of the publication of *Waverley*, 'I felt that something might be attempted for my own country, of the same kind with that which Miss Edgeworth so fortunately achieved for Ireland.'

Her friendships were many; her place in the world of English and Irish society was distinguished. Byron (little given to commending the women whom he did not make love to, or who did not make love to him) approved her. Scott, when personally a stranger to her, addressed her like an old friend and a sister. There is hardly a tourist of worth or note who has visited Ireland for the last fifty years without bearing testimony to her value and vivacity as one of a large and united home circle. She was small in stature, lively of address, and diffuse as a letter-writer. To sum up, it may be said that the changes and developments which have convulsed the world of imagination since Miss Edgeworth's career of authorship began, have not shaken her from her pedestal, nor blotted out her name from the honourable place which it must always keep in the records of European fiction.

The Annual Register of the year 1849

Charles Dickens 1812–1870

The interest of Charles Dickens's subject matter was remarked upon in a tone of surprise in obituary notices. His compassionate, thought-provoking descriptions of London life appealed to millions of readers in Britain and America, and to young and old his death was felt as deeply as the loss of a personal friend.

His creations have become naturalised, so to speak, among all classes of the community, and are familiar to every man, high or low. How many fine gentlemen and ladies, who never saw Pickwick or Sam Weller in the flesh, have laughed at their portraits of Charles Dickens. How many have been heartbroken at the sufferings of Oliver, been indignant at the brutality of Bill Sykes, wept over the fallen Nancy's cruel fate, and even sympathised with the terrible agony of Fagin in the condemned cell, who but for Charles Dickens would ever have known that such sorrows and crimes, such cruel wrongs, and such intensity of feeling existed in those lower depths of London life, far above which, like the golden gods of Epicurus, they lived in careless ease till this great apostle of the people touched their hearts and taught them that those inferior beings had hearts and souls of their own, and could be objects of sympathy as well as victims of neglect.

The Times, 11 June 1870

In the bar-room of a small public-house, in the back shop of a petty tradesman; in vulgar places of amusement – the gallery of a theatre or a free-and-easy concert-saloon, where smoking and drinking go on with the singing and dancing; in the police court, among the crowd of defendants or complainants, their loquacious witnesses or sympathising comrades, through whom the attorney's clerk and the official constable elbow their way to find the person they want; in the swarm of a parasitical population, honest and dishonest, some respectably and usefully industrious, some pretentious imposters or vicious mendicants, some downright swindlers or thieves, all clinging to the body of a rich old city and sucking it for their daily food, or teasing it with their inveterate tricks; here it was that the lively curiosity of Dickens and his keen enjoyment of the ridiculous delighted to revel. He loved to exhibit the warts and wens, the distorted toes and fingers, the bald or scrubby patches of hair, the broken teeth, the crooked back, the voice cracked or hoarse, the bleared and blinking eyes, the pimple on the nose, the halting awkwardness in the deportment, the sordid stains on the apparel of our hard-living race; but he did this in the spirit of compassion. He did with the pen what some of the old Dutch painters – Ostade, and Teniers, and Jan Steen – had done with the pencil, revealing not only the picturesque effects, but the interesting moral characteristics, that lie in the commonest and even the basest forms of plebian life.

The Illustrated London News, 18 June 1870

John Thadeus Delane *1817–1879*

Delane was editor of *The Times* from 1841 to 1877.

It is curiously said that most Englishmen accept the glorious phenomenon of sunrise on the authority of the poets who describe it and the astronomers who prove it, for they have never seen it themselves, except now and then on the walls of the Royal Academy. For nearly half the year Mr. Delane saw it every morning, not after what it is a mockery to call his night's rest, but before it.

The Times, 25 November 1879

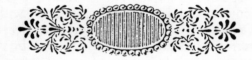

Thomas Carlyle 1795–1881

In April 1881, two months after his death, a memoir of Carlyle appeared in *Macmillan's Magazine*. The author was Mrs Oliphant, the novelist and friend of Mrs Carlyle, and her account was prompted by the posthumous publication of Carlyle's *Reminiscences*.

In late-Victorian England Carlyle was not only acknowledged as a historian of vision and great literary power but revered as a sage. To call upon him at his house in Chelsea and to experience his renowned ability to discourse for hours on end became for men of letters an essential part of a visit to London. Chronic dyspepsia and the strain of creative work made him often cantankerous and rude, but for those who found him in poor humour there was the compensation of taking tea with his wife, whose sharp wit and sociable nature made her the centre of a circle of her own.

For all their undoubted affection for each other and admiration for each other's qualities, Thomas and Jane were an ill-matched pair. When, after years of ill health and the strain of living with him, Jane Carlyle died suddenly in 1866 while out for a drive in her carriage, her husband was stricken with grief and remorse. In search of consolation he wrote *Reminiscences*, a long maudlin work of self-criticism, setting down in detail the story of their life together.

Mrs Oliphant continued to call on Carlyle after Jane's death and the following passage from her memoir describes her last meeting with him.

> I found him alone, seated in that room, which to him, as to me, was still her room, and full of sugges-tions of her – a place in which he was still a super-fluous figure, never entirely domiciled and at home. Few people are entirely unacquainted with that char-acteristic figure, so worn and feeble, yet never losing its marked identity; his shaggy hair falling rather wildly about his forehead, his vigorous grizzly beard, his keen eyes gleaming from below that overhanging ridge of forehead, from under the shaggy caverns of his eyebrows; his deep-toned complexion, almost of an orange-red, like that of an out-door labourer, a

119

man exposed to wind and storm and much 'knitting of his brows under the glaring sun;' his gaunt, tall, tottering figure always wrapped in a long, dark grey coat or dressing-gown, the cloth of which, carefully and with difficulty sought out for him, had cost doubly dear both in money and trouble, in that he insisted upon its being entirely genuine cloth, without a suspicion of *shoddy;* his large, bony, tremulous hands, long useless for any exertion – scarcely, with a great effort, capable of carrying a cup to his lips. There he sat, as he had sat for all these years, since *her* departure left him stranded, a helpless man amid the wrecks of life. Ever courteous, full of old-fashioned politeness, he would totter to his feet to greet his visitor, even in that last languor. This time he was not uncheerful. It was inevitable that he should repeat that prevailing sentiment always in his mind about the death for which he was waiting; but he soon turned to a very different subject. In this old house, never before brightened by the sight of children, a baby had been born, a new Thomas Carlyle, the child of his niece and nephew, as near to him as it was possible for any living thing in the third generation to be. He spoke of it with tender amusement and wonder. It was 'a bonnie little manikin', a perfectly good and well-conditioned child, taking life sweetly, and making no more than the inevitable commotion in the tranquil house. There had been fears as to how he would take this innocent intruder, whether its advent might disturb or annoy him; on the contrary, it gave him a half-amused and genial pleasure, tinged with his prevailing sentiment, yet full of natural satisfaction in the continuance of his name and race. This little life coming unconscious across the still scene in which he attended the slow arrival of death, awoke in its most intimate and touching form the self-reference and comparison which was habitual to him. It was curious, he said, very curious! thus to contrast the newcomer with 'the parting guest.' It was a new view to him, bringing together the exit and the entrance with a force both humorous and solemn. The 'bonnie little manikin,' one would imagine, pushed him softly, tenderly, with baby hands not much less serviceable than his own, towards the verge. The old man looked on with a half-incredulous, and wondering mixture of pain and pleasure, bursting into one of those convulsions of broken laughter, sudden and strange, which were part of his habitual utterance. Thus I left him, scarcely restrained by his weakness from his old habit of accompanying me to the door. For he was courtly in those little traditions of politeness, and had often conducted me downstairs upon his arm, when I was fain to support him instead of accepting his tremulous guidance.

And that was my last sight of Thomas Carlyle.

Macmillan's Magazine, April 1881

Mrs Craik 1826–1887

Authoress, remembered especially for *John Halifax, Gentleman*, a novel illustrating the highest of Victorian middle-class ideals.

She was democratic. She believed in the nobility of man as man, and looked upon condition, circumstance, or birth as an accident which ought not to determine his ultimate position. Her ideal man, John Halifax, carried about with him an old Greek Testament, in which, after the name of an ancestor, was the inscription 'Gentleman'. Such a charter she held to be the undeniable possession of every human being.

The Athenaeum, 22 October 1887

Alfred, Lord Tennyson 1809–1892

The son of a clergyman in affluent circumstances, Tennyson's life from first to last was seen by others as a singularly happy one. At the age when most boys were beginning to labour over the grindstone of Latin verse, he was writing poetry that was full of promise for the future. By all accounts, this poet 'of the feelings and affections', who lived to a grand old age, had an enviable life.

> He meditated and laboured over his gracefully-polished work; each melodious line and measured couplet was the deliberate expression of his feelings; he wrote slowly and published leisurely. The rich exuberances of fancy were lopped and pruned; his deepest sentiments were seldom obscure; the loftiest flights of his philosophical mysticism rarely carried him beyond reach of the perceptions of his intelligent worshippers. In short, his methods were the very opposite of those of the greatest of his rivals, and he had his full reward. His genius ripened steadily and surely. His reputation increased with the appreciative and sympathetic, as his popularity was widely extended among the crowd. With a single exception, which was soon forgotten or forgiven, each publication was as warmly welcomed as it had been eagerly expected. In the enjoyment of ample means, absolute master of his time and of his arrangements, he made his favourite recreation his regular occupation, writing just as much or as little as he pleased. He led the easy life of a country gentleman as he understood it, drawing inspiration for his scenery and his minutely-exquisite painting of nature from the lanes and downs that surrounded his dwellings. He had the choice of two country residences in the fairest districts of southern England; he had books at will as the companions of his solitude when he cared for solitude; and we may add, though it sounds something of a bathos, he found unfailing solace in an inexhaustible tobacco-jar.
>
> *The Times,* 7 October 1892

Longevity

Grow old along with me!
The best is yet to be,
The last of life, for which the first was made;
Our times are in His hand
Who saith, 'A whole I planned,
Youth shows but half; trust God: see all,
nor be afraid!'

Rabbi ben Ezra by Robert Browning
(1812–1889)

Jane Hook and Sarah Wood died 1731

In the town of Belfast in Ireland one Jane Hook, 112 yeares of age had lately all her old stumps drove out by a new set of teeth; which were more welcome, because the Account affirms her Appetite and other faculties are as good as when she was but 20.

From Ogher in the same kingdom, came an History of the death of one Sarah Wood, who after having three or four children regularly went seven years with child, and was at last deliver'd of a dead one at her navel, together with some bones of another child; after which she recover'd, went abroad, and perform'd all offices of life with pretty good Health; which is attested by Mr. William M'Ivers, an Irish Physician.

The Gentleman's Magazine, July 1731

William Haseling 1621–1733

Wm. Haseling, the oldest pensioner in Chelsea College, aged 112 years, and 6 months. He was in the Parliament Army at Edgehill; serv'd under K. William in Ireland, and the D. of Marlborough in Flanders. He married and buried 2 wives since he was 100, and the 3d, who survives him, he married about 2 years ago. Besides his Allowance from the College, he had a Crown a week from the D. of Richmond, and another from Sir Robert Walpole.

The Gentleman's Magazine, February 1733

Janet Gordon 1653–1753

The widow of Dr George Middleton, Principal of King's College, Aberdeen, by whom she had fourteen sons and four daughters. She died at the age of one hundred years ten months.

> An affectionate wife,
> An indulgent mother,
> A sincere friend,
> An agreeable companion.

> In domestic concerns a great œconomist;
> Too good to be churlish,
> Too wise to be prodigal.
> Of exemplary piety,
> And universal benevolence.
> Happy in a calm and dispassionate temper,
> She bore the accidents of human life,
> As became a Christian.

> Art thou surprised at her great age, O Reader!
> I blame thee not – reflect with me
> On the probable causes.

> 'Twas not an indolent life,
> She had eighteen children,
> 'Twas not a continual sunshine,
> She felt the misfortunes of others.
> 'Twas a chearful temper,
> A clear conscience,
> Moderate exercise,
> And a temperate life.

Aberdeen Intelligencer, February 1753

125

Francis Ange *died* 1767

In Somerset county, Maryland, in a very advanced age, Francis Ange. A gentleman of that province, some years ago having occasioned to ride in the neighbourhood where this man lived, and hearing of his great age, had the curiosity to go and see him. In a letter to a friend of his in Boston, dated Aug. 9. 1764, he gives the following account of him, as he had it from the man himself: That he was born at Stratford upon Avon, in Warwickshire, England: That his father was a cutler by trade: That he could remember K. Charles I being beheaded, as he was then a pretty big boy: That he went to that country in a ship from Parkgate, called *the Great Bengal,* and served his time with one Nicholas Demar, on Rappahannock. The gentleman says, that at that time he was not less than 130 years of age, had scarce a wrinkle in his face, had thick black hair, with very few gray hairs interspersed, and that his wife, who was then about 80, had a son by him not above 27 years of age.

The Scots Magazine, September 1767

Edward Drinker 1680–1782

Born in Philadelphia, Drinker lived to the age of 103 in that city, shortly before his death being apprised of the birth of a grandchild to one of his grandchildren.

The life of this man is marked with several circumstances which perhaps have seldom occurred in the life of an individual: he saw and heard more of those events which are measured by time than have ever been seen or heard by any man since the age of the patriarchs: he saw the same spot of earth in the course of his life covered with wood and bushes, and the receptacle of beasts and birds of prey, afterwards become the seat of a city not only the first in wealth and arts in the *new*, but rivalling in both many of the first cities in the *old* world. He saw regular streets where he once pursued a hare: he saw churches rising up on morasses where he had often heard the croaking of frogs: he saw wharfs and warehouses where he had often seen Indian savages draw fish from the river for their daily subsistence; and he saw ships of every size and use in those streams where he had been used to see nothing but Indian canoes: he saw a stately edifice filled with legislators astonishing the world with their wisdom and virtue on the same spot probably where he had seen an Indian council-fire: he saw the first treaty ratified between the newly confederated powers of America, and the ancient monarchy of France, with all the formalities of parchment and seals, on the same spot probably where he once saw William Penn ratify his first and last treaty with the Indians without the formalities of pen, ink, or paper: he saw all the intermediate stages through which a people pass from the most simple to the most complicated degrees of civilization: he saw the beginning and end of the empire of Great Britain in *Pennsylvania*.

He had been the subject of seven crowned heads, and afterwards died a citizen of the newly created republic of America. The number of his sovereigns, and his long habits of submission to them, did not extinguish the love of republican liberty which is natural to the mind of man in its healthy state. He embraced the liberties and independence of America in his withered arms, and triumphed in the last years of his life in the salvation of his country.

The Gentleman's Magazine, May 1783

William Riddel *died 1788*

Lately, at Selkirk, aged 116, William Riddel. In the early part of his life he dealt deep in the smuggling and drinking of brandy, and was always so fond of good ale, that he had been often heard to declare he had never taken a single draught of water. He could never be called an habitual drinker, but frequently fell into intemperate rambles of several days continuance, and even after he was 90; he at one time drank a fortnight before he went to bed. He married his third wife when he was 95; and retained his memory and judgement to the last. For the last two years of his life he subsisted chiefly on ale and spirits mixed with a little bread.

The Scots Magazine, July 1788

Mrs Price *died 1791*

At a very advanced age, Mrs. Price, mother of Thomas Price, esq., formerly of Rushulme. She had experienced great vicissitudes of fortune, which she bore with uncommon fortitude and christian resignation. She was confined to her bed nearly twelve months, and, what is very extraordinary, during that time she cut two teeth; and her hair which had been grey many years, changed to its natural colour.

The Gentleman's Magazine, March 1791

J. Reside 1706–1808

It would be interesting to know how the writer of this obituary would compare 'the pampered and voluptuous sons of the present day' with those of our own day.

> On Thursday, the 26t ult. Mr. J. Reside, of Drumaul, farmer, aged 102 years. His long life adds another to the many we have upon record, of the effects of temperance on the human frame. Temperate in all his meals, he enjoyed almost uninterrupted good health till near his last. He was, perhaps, never intoxicated during his whole life: and his manner of living more resembled the ancients than the pampered and voluptuous sons of the present day.

> *The Examiner*, June 1808

James Carroll 1711–1817

At Bulogurteen (Kilkenny) aged 106, James Carroll. A few years ago an elder brother of his died aged 117, who was attended to the grave by 80 children and grand-children, the least of whose ages was above 50 years, and a son of his now alive who is near 100 years old, and enjoys good health and the perfect possession of his faculties.

The Gentleman's Magazine, December 1817

Musicians and Singers

He is dead, the sweet musician!
He the sweetest of all singers!
He has gone from us for ever,
He has moved a little nearer
To the Master of all music,
To the Master of all singing!
O my brother, Chibiabos!

Hiawatha's Lamentation
by Henry Wadsworth Longfellow
(1807–1882)

Sir John Dutton *died 1743*

Sir John Dutton, of Sherbourn, Gloucestershire. This family has a right to license the minstrels in the county of Chester; for which a court is kept every Midsummer-day, when every minstrel summoned pays 4d. 2q. and every whore that follows her calling 4d.

The Scots Magazine, February 1743

George Frederick Handel *1856–1759*

When complimented by Lord Kinnoull upon the splendid entertainment which he had recently given an audience with his *Messiah,* Handel is reputed to have replied: 'My Lord, I should be sorry if I only entertained them. I wish to make them better.'

April 12, George Frederick Handel, esq; as great a genius perhaps in music, as the late Mr. Pope was in poetry. The musical composition of the one being as expressive of the passions, as the happy versification of the other excelled in harmony. Mr. Handel was born in the year 1685, in Germany; but had spent the greater part of his time in England, where the encouragement given to his seraphic composition was a distinguishing instance of the English taste for the fine arts.

Catalogue and Review of New Books and Pamphlets, 1759

Giacobbe Cervetto 1682?–1783

Popularizer of the violoncello in England, Cervetto was conspicuous in the Drury Lane orchestra for the ostentatiously large diamond ring he wore on his bow hand. It caught the light when he played and attracted as much notice as his prominent nose. He died, aged at least 101, at Friburg's snuff shop in the Haymarket.

This extraordinary character in the musical world was 102 years old in November last. He came to England in the winter of the hard frost, and was then an old man. He soon after was engaged to play the bass at Drury-lane theatre, and continued in that employment till a season or two previous to Mr. Garrick's retiring from the stage. One evening when Mr. Garrick was performing the character of Sir John Brute, during the drunkards muttering and dosing till he falls fast asleep in the chair (the audience being most profoundly silent and attentive to the admirable performer), Cervetto (in the orchestra) uttered a very loud and immoderately-lengthened yawn! The moment Garrick was off the stage he sent for the musician, and with considerable warmth reprimanded him for so ill-timed a symptom of somnolency, when the modern Naso, with great address, reconciled Garrick to him in a trice, by saying, with a shrug, 'I beg ten thousand pardon! but I always do *so ven I am ver mush please!*' Mr. Cervetto was a constant frequenter of the Orange Coffee-house, and was distinguished among his friends of the galleries by the name of *Nosey*.

The Gentleman's Magazine, January 1783

Signor Marchesi *died 1792*

At Milan, the celebrated vocal performer, Marchesi. It is said that he fell a victim to the jealousy of an Italian nobleman, whose wife was suspected of too strong an attachment to the unfortunate warbler. As a singer, Marchesi was certainly one of the first that ever appeared in this country; for taste, expression, science and vast compass of voice. Poison, administered with the usual skill and dispatch of the Italians, is said to have produced his unhappy exit.

The Gentleman's Magazine, March 1792

Charles Norris *died* 1793

A contemporary described Charles Norris as 'an excellent musician, and master of several instruments; but while academic indolence prevented his making any exertions on them, academic ale, by degrees, injured his voice, and he at last excited pity instead of applause'.

At Imley-hall, near Stourbridge, in Worcestershire, the seat of Lord Dudley and Ward, Charles Norris, Mus. Bac. organist of St. John's College and of Christchurch, in the University of Oxford, well known in the musical world as a capital singer. The ill state of Mr. N's health, for some time before this dissolution, considerably injured him in his musical engagements. At the last Abbey commemoration, such was his debility that he could not hold the book from which he sang; his whole frame was agitated by a nervous tremor, and that voice which, in the plenitude of health, was wont to inspire rapture, excited pity. Of this failure he was too sensible; and, anxious to support that professional fame which constitutes so large a portion of the happiness of those who excel in any of the liberal arts, he engaged himself at the late Birmingham music-meeting, where, on the first day, he was unsuccessful, and omitted an air; but on the last night his exertions dazzled, astonished, enraptured! he excelled himself even in his happiest days, and the theatre rang with just applause. The effort, however, was fatal; for like Strada's nightingale, he sang himself to death. In ten short days after this too violent, though successful struggle for fame, 'deaf *was* the prais'd ear, and mute the tuneful tongue!'

The Gentleman's Magazine, October 1793

John Davy 1763–1824

Composer whose musical talents manifested themselves early in life.

> Before he was quite six years old, a neighbouring
> smith, into whose house he used frequently to run,
> lost between twenty and thirty horse-shoes; diligent
> search was made after them for many days, but to no
> purpose. Soon after, the smith heard some musical
> sounds, which seemed to come from the upper part of
> the house; and having listened a sufficient time to be
> convinced that his ears did not deceive him, he went
> up stairs, where he discovered the young musician
> and his property between the ceiling of the garret and
> the thatched roof. He had selected eight horse-shoes,
> out of more than twenty, to form a complete octave;
> had suspended each of them by a single cord, clear
> from the wall; and, with a small iron rod, was amus-
> ing himself by imitating Crediton chimes.

The Annual Register of the year 1824

John Bruce died 1847

We learn from a gentleman in Edinburgh, that
among the latest victims of the fever at present raging
in that city, was John Bruce, or 'John of Skye', for
some years the Highland piper at Abbotsford. In his
best days John was a fine athletic man. Latterly,
however, the poor fellow got wild and unsettled,
imagined himself a descendant of Robert Bruce, and
hinted at his pretentions to the throne, which only
his regard for 'the young lady Queen' prevented him
from asserting. He still wandered about, old and
indigent, playing the pipes which he had received

from Sir Walter. Though more than 70 years of age, and subjected to much hardship and privation, John of Skye walked erect and had a military air to the last. There was no relation to claim the poor piper's remains, and his body was sent to one of the dissecting rooms. A medical student purchased for a trifle the bagpipes which he was so proud to bear as a gift of the great magician, and with which he had once charmed 'high dames and mighty earls' in hall and green wood.

Douglas Jerrold's Weekly Newspaper, 11 December 1847

Frederick de Landre *1795–1879*

Swedish musician who 'subsisted rather neatly than handsomely' by teaching the flute in London.

He was harmless, fond of an immense queue wig in full powder, and, to the last moment, wore a diamond ring of tolerable water. These are propensities common to foreigners.

The Gentleman's Magazine, January 1800

Jenny Lind *1820–1887*

'The Swedish Nightingale', as she was called in Britain and America, was acclaimed as a singer with a voice of 'touching sincerity', but it was the gentleness and sweetness of her nature that made her the object of popular adoration.

It is not remembered that she was considered a great beauty; the winning quality of her face and presence did not reside in her physical features, in the blue eyes and fair hair of her race, or in the moderately well-proportioned form, but in the look of womanly goodness and kindliness, and in the artless, spontaneous, unconscious play of mental moods, revealing a lovely spirit, which animated the countenance not less in ordinary conversation than in the height of dramatic action. While those who could judge of her capacities and attainments as a singer were profuse in laudations, the greater number of admirers were those who regarded her almost as a new personal revelation of moral grace in humanity, crediting her with purer and nobler sentiments than those of the generality of mankind. Doubtless there always were, and are, in every community many ladies quite as good as she; but people chose her for a type of amiability. Jenny Lind was worshipped as a heroine with the same kind of romantic enthusiasm that made Garibaldi, long afterwards, the hero of the people's imagination; and her name was cherished by hundreds of thousands of the poor and the working classes, in their humble homes and in the London streets, though none of them could see or hear the famous songstress, for it had become a symbol of that ideal humanity which stirs the deep affections of simple hearts. It is probable enough that no real personage who has been famous in our time actually merited such a degree of exaltation; but the phenomenon of this kind of worship has been witnessed in several instances, and proves the existence of a natural longing for something good and lovely to believe in, which is starved by the dullness and meanness of common life.

The Illustrated London News, 12 November 1887

Pedestrians

'I'm sure nobody walks much faster than I do!'
'He can't do that', said the King, 'or
else he'd have been here first.'

Alice Through the Looking-Glass
by Lewis Carroll (1832–1898)

Sir Hildebrand Jacob *1716–1786*

At Malvern-Wells, co. Worcester, aged 76, Sir Hildebrand Jacob, Bart. of Yewhall, co. Oxford. He succeeded his grandfather Sir John, 1740, his father, Hildebrand, having died in 1739. He was a very extraordinary character. As a general scholar, he was exceeded by few; in his knowledge of the Hebrew language he scarcely had an equal. In the earlier part of his life, one custom which he constantly followed was very remarkable. As soon as the roads became pretty good, and the fine weather began to set in, his man was ordered to pack up a few things in a portmanteau, and with these, his master and himself set off, without knowing whither they were going. When it drew towards evening, they enquired at the first village they saw, whether the great man in it was a lover of books, and had a fine library. If the answer was in the negative, they went on farther; if in the affirmative, Sir Hildebrand sent his compliments, that he was come to see him; and there he used to stay till time or curiosity induced him to move elsewhere. In this manner Sir Hildebrand had, very nearly, passed through the greatest part of England, without scarely ever sleeping at an inn, unless where the town or village did not afford one person in it civilized enough to be glad to see a gentleman and a scholar. He was buried at St. Anne's, Soho, on the 22nd.

The Gentleman's Magazine, October 1786

Simon Elderton 1695–1799

Lately, at Craikie, in the county of Durham at the advanced age of 104, Simon Elderton, a noted pedestrian. He resided many years in a neat stone cottage of his own building, every particle of which he had carried on his head, it being his practice to bring home, on every journey or message in which he was employed, the purest stone he could pick up for his purpose, till he had completed his collection. Although the motive ceased, the practice continued, as he imagined a weight on his head facilitated his walking. If anyone enquired the reason, he used facetiously to answer, 'Tis to keep my hat on.'

The Scots Magazine, March 1799

William Burridge died 1819

At Greenfield, near Ampthill, aged 90, Wm. Burridge, labourer; a rare instance of pedestrian servitude; having regularly, and punctual to his time, for 32 years, walked from his cottage to his circle of work, in Ampthill Park, averaging about seven miles a day, nearly 70,000 miles: which is almost three times the circumference of the globe.

The Gentleman's Magazine, July 1819

William Hurst *died 1823*

Aged 80, Mr. Wm. Hurst. He had been a famed pedestrian, having visited most parts of England and Scotland on foot; nor did he confine his walks to his own country only, but visited many parts of the Continent, such as Flanders, France, Portugal, Gibraltar, the island of Malta, &c. His usual beverage and food when travelling was tea, bread and butter. His walks were long and rapid – walking from Margate to London, and back again, in two days, spending in the journey only a few pence. In one of his tours he was shut in a fort, when it was besieged by the French; he continued there during the siege, and was taken prisoner when it capitulated; but was set at liberty when the object of his pursuit was known.

The Gentleman's Magazine, August 1823

Dorothy Ripley *died 1832*

Dorothy Ripley, who lately died in Virginia, aged about 64, says the Richmond compiler, was 'perhaps the most extraordinary woman in the world'. This lady 'crossed the Atlantic 19 times – 11 times since 1825 – travelled no doubt more than any other woman in the world – perhaps 100,000 miles – preached to hundreds and thousands of nearly all classes under the sun! Her travelling expenses must have cost $20,000! And whom did it come from? Perhaps from the poor and needy. We enter our solemn protest against all such extraordinary examples. Hannah More and Hannah Adams have benefited the world more by a single day's labor, by staying at home, than Dorothy Ripley, by travelling her whole life.

The Boston Morning Post, 24 January 1832

Physicians and Nurses

Cur'd yesterday of my disease,
I died last night of my physician.

The Remedy Worse than the Disease
by Matthew Prior (1664–1721)

Dr William Hunter *1718–1783*

Dr William Hunter founded and endowed the Hunterian Museum in Glasgow, which contains collections of minerals, shells, rare books, coins and medals and other antiquities as well as anatomical specimens and curiosities assembled by him in the course of his life as a surgeon and lecturer in anatomy.

> To consider him as a teacher, is to view him in his most amiable character; perspicuity, unaffected modesty, and a desire of being useful, were his peculiar characteristics; and, of all others, he was most happy in blending the *utile* with the *dulce*, by introducing apposite and pleasing stories, to illustrate and enliven the most abstruse and jejune parts of anatomy; thus fixing the attention of the volatile and the giddy, and enriching the minds of all with useful knowledge.
>
> *The Gentleman's Magazine*, April 1783

Dr Edward Jenner *1749–1823*

Until Dr Jenner's discovery of the smallpox vaccine, it was calculated that in the British Isles alone 40,000 people perished from the disease annually: one fourteenth of all that were born died of it. 'Nature had given him great genius, vast sagacity, much inclination, and great ardour in the prosecution of his subjects of Natural History, Physiology, and Pathology.' He was much admired and respected as a physician, and in private as a man of refinement and 'hospitable habits'.

For some years before his death, Dr. Jenner's purse and his table demonstrated his public spirit, his hospitable habits, and his unassuming intercourse with society. In his house-keeping nothing was gaudy, but all was good. The cookery was tastefully and fashionably set out; the wines, commonly five or six kinds, old and of fine flavour. The conversation was lively, and generally of a philosophical turn. At a striking innocent trait of character, the Philosopher, as a keen observer, would smile cheerfully, but the writer of this never saw him indulge in what is called a horse-laugh.

The Gentleman's Magazine, February 1823

Eleanor Job *died 1823*

Eleanor Job, in Church-court, in the parish of St. Giles, at the very advanced age of 105 years. In the first contest between this country and America, she accompanied her husband, who was a soldier of artillery, to the latter country, where she attended with the army in every campaign that took place, as principal nurse in what was called at that time the flying hospital. Her intrepidity and humanity were equally proverbial with the army, for she had been often known to rush forward at the cannon's mouth, on the field of battle, to assist in the dressing of the wounded soldiers, with whom she was held in such regard that she was familiarly known among them by the name of 'Good Mother Job'. At the battle of Quebec she was particularly conspicuous in her heroic exertions to relieve the wounded, and was the person selected on that occasion to prepare for embalment the remains of the brave, gallant, and lamented Wolfe.

The Gentleman's Magazine, Supplement to 1823

Sir James Simpson *1811–1870*

From an account of Simpson's funeral, a comment on the loss that would be felt in Edinburgh at the death of one of her most illustrious citizens who had pioneered the use of chloroform as an anaesthetic.

We learn from one who had the best opportunities of knowing, that such was Sir James Simpson's power of attracting to the city the high-born and the wealthy as patients, that £80,000 a year would hardly cover the aggregate loss individually borne by hotel proprietors, lodging-house keepers, and tradesmen.

The Lancet, 21 May 1870

Sir Henry Holland 1788–1873

'Sir Henry was essentially *homme de société*', it was noted in an obituary of the well-known London physician published in *The Lancet*. 'Having early in life gained his footing as a practitioner among the 'upper ten', it was his pleasure – perhaps his foible, to be on intimate, or apparently intimate, terms with everyone of note. Whether in actual medical attendance or not, upon any sick celebrity, Sir Henry's carriage was to be seen waiting at the door, and he always had the latest bulletin of the invalid's health.' *The Times* drew the attention of its readers to the important rôle of men of medicine in attendance upon people in high places.

He had associated in every capital in Europe with all that is, or was, most eminent for rank, birth, genius, wit, learning, and accomplishment. He could call every leading statesman of the United States and every President for the last half-century his friend. In his professional capacity, besides a long list of royal and princely patients, he had the honour and deep responsibility of prescribing for six Prime Ministers of England, besides Chancellors of the Exchequer, Secretaries of State, Presidents of the Council, Chief Justices, and Lord Chancellors.

We say 'deep responsibility,' because it is difficult to over-estimate the influence of health on statesmanship, on the administration of justice, or on the general conduct of affairs. Although the fact of Pitt's illness behind the Speaker's chair, during the speech to which he made his famous reply in 1783, did not impair his eloquence, the collapse of the Ministry formed by Lord Chatham in 1766 was certainly owing to suppressed gout. There were three occasions – Borodino, the third day of Dresden, and Waterloo – on which the eagle eye of Napoleon was perceptibly dimmed by indigestion or physical suffering. When Lord Tenterden's stomach was out of order – as it generally was after a City dinner, from his extreme fondness for turtle – woe to the unlucky junior who cited an inapplicable case, and still greater woe to the prisoner who had the misfortune to appear before him in the criminal court.

The Times, 31 October 1873

Dr Hugh Martin died 1874

Wednesday last died, in this city Dr. Hugh Martin whose success in the cure of the cancers had rendered him justly celebrated throughout the continent. We do not learn whether the important secret of the preparation of his remedy for that fatal malady, has died with this gentleman or not.

The Independent Gazette or *The New York Journal Revived,* 5 February 1874

Florence Nightingale 1820–1910

Florence Nightingale died in London on 13 August in her 91st year. Two days later *The Times* in the third leading article evaluated the many services she had rendered to her country: 'There is no parallel record of a combination of the highest feminine tact with the highest masculine energy, perseverance, and determination.' She understood, as none before, 'the futility of any struggle against disease which was not based upon a recognition of its physical causes, and of the uselessness of even hoping for improvement as long as these causes continued in operation', and she was 'guided by the light of such knowledge, without giving heed either to the specious excuses or the despairing cries of routine officialism'. She also 'greatly rehabilitated the private soldier in the estimation of civilians' by her account of their dignity and gentleness in the Crimea.

The same day, in addition to the article, appeared a four-column obituary of 'the Lady-in-Chief', quoting the legendary story of the veneration in which she was held by the soldiers.

> Her zeal, her devotion, and her perseverance would yield to no rebuff and to no difficulty. She went steadily and unwearyingly about her work with a judgement, a self-sacrifice, a courage, a tender sympathy, and withal a quiet and unostentatious demeanour that won the hearts of all who were not prevented by official prejudice from appreciating the nobility of her work and character. One poor fellow wrote home:– 'She would speak to one and nod and smile to many more; but she could not do it to all, you know. We lay there by hundreds; but we could kiss her shadow as it fell, and lay our heads on the pillow again, content'.
>
> *The Times*, 15 August 1910

Lord Lister *1827–1912*

Before Lister's researches into antiseptics, the good wrought by surgeons performing operations with the aid of anaesthetics was too often counteracted by the evils of infection. He 'raised English surgery to a pinnacle from which not even the presumptuous ignorance of politicians will be able to take it down', claimed *The Lancet* triumphantly.

> Even in private houses, and, as it seemed, amid surroundings of the most favourable kind, the operations which, because they could be rendered painless, were freely and hopefully undertaken, were in a lamentable proportion of cases rendered of no account by death; while the surgical wards of many hospitals became veritable pest-houses, from which escape with life could hardly be regarded as probable. It seems scarcely credible to-day, but it is none the less true, that only half a century ago it was gravely proposed that surgical hospitals should be temporary buildings, which should be destroyed by fire, as dangerous nuisances, after the fulfilment of two or three years of existence, or as soon as gangrene became of common occurrence among their inmates.

The Lancet, 17 February 1912

Royals and
Rulers

The glories of our blood and state
Are shadows, not substantial things;
There is no armour against fate;
Death lays his icy hand on kings:
Sceptre and crown,
Must tumble down,
And in the dust be equal made
With the poor crooked scythe and spade.

The Contention of Ajax and Ulysses
by James Shirley (1596–1666)

Louis XIV *1638–1715*

French soldier, statesman and writer, the fame of the Duc de Saint-Simon rests on his *Memoirs* in which he described and commented on French affairs and the French court over a period of about thirty years, spanning the reigns of Louis XIV and Louis XV. Although alive to the good qualities of Louis XIV, the Sun King, he mourned their absence where affairs of state were concerned.

He wished to reign by himself. His jealousy on this point unceasingly became weakness. He reigned, indeed, in little things; the great he could not reach: even in the former, too, he was often governed. The superior ability of his early ministers and his early government soon wearied him. He liked nobody to be in any way superior to him. Thus, he chose his ministers, not for their knowledge, but for their ignorance; not for their capacity but for their want of it. He liked to form them, as he said: liked to teach them even the most trifling things. It was the same with his generals. He took credit to himself for instructing them; wished it to be thought that from his cabinet he commanded and directed all his armies. Naturally fond of trifles, he increasingly occupied himself with the most petty details of his troops, his household, his mansions; would even instruct his cooks who received, like novices, lessons they had known by heart for years. This vanity, this unmeasured and unreasonable love of admiration, was his ruin. His ministers, his generals, his mistresses, his courtiers, soon perceived his weakness. They praised him with emulation and spoiled him. Praises, or to say truth, flattery, pleased him to such an extent that the coarsest was well received, the vilest even better relished.

Saint-Simon, *Memoirs* (1715)

His Majesty, John I,
King of Dalkey *died* 1788

The Irish have long been famed for their eccentric characters and behaviour. 'John I' introduced the burlesque election of a king to Dalkey, a small port and watering place in Co. Dublin, and until the end of the eighteenth century, Dalkey was notorious for this mock ceremony which became invested with a certain political significance.

At Dublin, his Majesty John the First, King of Dalkey, and the adjacent Isles. His remains were borne, in royal pomp, through the city, and interred with the usual splendour and solemnity. – In the case of the above personage we have a strong instance of the height to which the human imagination may be raised. Moving in the middle sphere of life, he was persuaded that he was actually a monarch, and was alive to all that tender solicitude which the father of a people should ever feel. A society, called The Kingdom of Dalkey, had appointed him their sovereign, and annually attended him to visit his territories. Complimented frequently with the title of Majesty, the idea got possession of all his senses, and absolutely turned his brain; so that, for a year and a half past, his residence was Swift's Hospital. Before his decease, his time was occupied in arranging the affairs of his kingdom. He desired that all his great officers of state might be continued. 'My Chancellor,' said he, 'never degraded his dignity by bargaining for places and pensions; my Attorney-General never pleaded in soul dishonour's cause, nor burned his fingers with attachments; my Primates and Archbishops have more grace than what they derive from titles; my Council was honest; and if there is truth in wine, they possess more truth than any council in Europe: let them all continue,' said he, with an air of fortitude and composure. 'But, my crown!' – here he was the man – his firmness forsook him, and he seemed averse to die, not from the fear of death, but from the thought of leaving his crown behind him. As the big tear trickled from his eye, he exclaimed, 'Let my crown be left to the election of my subjects.' So much for his public conduct; in private, he was distinguished for sincerity, chearfulness, and a love of social mirth. Poor fellow! he had no gall to overflow; and we may say with Sterne, if a nettle should grow upon his grave, it ought to be plucked away; for there was no humour in the temperament of his body or mind which could give nourishment to so noxious a weed.

The Scots Magazine, December 1788

Louis XVI *1754–1793*

The writer of this obituary seems, like many of his contemporaries, to have been influenced by the manner in which Louis XVI died. Weak in character and mentally dull, the courage and dignity which Louis XVI showed during his trial and on the scaffold has left him a better reputation than he deserves.

HIS MOST CHRISTIAN MAJESTY LOUIS THE SIXTEENTH. Born Aug. 23, 1754, he was 39 years old. He began his reign May 10, 1774; was driven from the Thuilleries, Aug. 10, 1791; thrown into prison on the 14th, and dethroned Sept. 22 following. He had reigned 18 years and 3 months. – That his death is one of the most atrocious acts that ever disgraced the annals of the world; that the manner in which it was perpetrated, with all the circumstances associated to the horrid catastrophe, aggravates the guilt; and that the ruling men in France are monsters, such as civilized society never yet beheld; are opinions which the splendid sense of Justice, and the benign spirit of Humanity, that form the glorious and elevating distinction of the British people, will impress on every mind throughout our happy country. The virtues of this murdered King were his ruin. He has suffered for having been a tyrant; and, had he been a tyrant, he would not have suffered. He would then have proceeded in that career of uncontrolled sovereignty, and have commanded a continuance of that submission, which waited upon the will of his royal predecessors; but, in fact, there was not a tyrannic principle in his character, which overflowed with benevolence and paternal affection for his people.

The Gentleman's Magazine, January 1793

Mr MacGillivray *died* 1793

Improbably enough, this son of a Scotsman was to end his life as a Creek chief. The Creeks, so-called because of the many creeks and rivulets which ran through their country, were a confederacy of North American Indians who formerly occupied most of Alabama and Georgia. Brave fighters, they were involved some twenty years after Mr MacGillivray's death in the Creek War, which resulted in the cession to the United States Government of most of their country.

At Pensacola, Mr. MacGillivray, a Creek chief, very much lamented by those who knew him best. There happened to be at that time at Pensacola, a numerous band of Creeks, who watched his illness with the most marked anxiety; and when his death was announced to them, and while they followed him to the grave, it is impossible for words to describe the loud screams of real woe which they vented in their unaffected grief. He was, by his father's side, a Scotchman, of the respectable family of Drumnaglass, in Invernesshire. The vigour of his mind overcame the disadvantages of an education had in the wilds of America; and he was well acquainted with all the most useful European sciences. In the latter part of his life he composed, with great care, the history of several classes of the original inhabitants of America; and this he intended to present to Professor Robertson, for publication in the next edition of his History. The European and the American writer are now no more; and the MSS of the latter, it is feared, have perished, for the Indians adhere to their custom of destroying whatever inanimate objects a dead friend most delighted in. It is only since Mr. MacGillvray had influence amongst them, that they have suffered the slaves of a deceased master to live.

The Gentleman's Magazine, August 1793

Edward, Duke of Kent 1767–1820

Fourth son of George III, the Duke of Kent was the father of Queen Victoria. After her birth he removed to Sidmouth and there, before she was one year old, he died from inflammation of the lungs. Returning from a walk in the beautiful environs of the town, he was advised by his companion, Captain Conroy, to change his boots and stockings which were wet, 'but this he did not do till he dressed for dinner, being attracted by the smiles of his infant Princess, with whom he sat for a considerable time in fond parental dalliance'.

> The Duke of Kent was tall in stature, of a manly and noble presence. His manners were affable, condescending, dignified, and engaging; his conversation animated; his information varied and copious; his memory exact and retentive; his intellectual powers quick, strong, and masculine, he resembled the King in many of his tastes and propensities; he was an early riser, a close economist of his time; temperate in eating; indifferent to wine, though a lover of society; and heedless of slight indisposition, from confidence in the general strength of his constitution; a kind master, a punctual and courteous correspondent, a steady friend and an affectionate brother.

> *The News,* 30 January 1820

George III 1738–1820

Within a week of the death of his son, the Duke of Kent, the demise of the King was announced from Windsor Castle. *The News* published a damning account of his reign – in the course of which England had lost America and accumulated a vast national debt – and passed the following verdict on the deceased sovereign.

> The character of a dead King, is public property: it is

157

the awful material of History; and as such we have treated it. The inducements to flattery die with those who are flattered: and slander is stript of its motives. The late KING, in common life, would have been regarded as a good, but a very common, man – a perfect sample of the *million*.

The News, 13 February 1820

Queen of the Sandwich Islands died 1824

In June 1824 London was startled by the arrival of Kamehameha II, King of the Sandwich Islands, accompanied by his wife and attendants. A 'grand entertainment' was given for them by the Foreign Secretary Mr Canning at Gloucester Lodge, where the Queen, who was six foot two inches in height, made an impression by appearing partly in European and partly in native attire. 'Their tawny Majesties' attended a performance at the Covent Garden Theatre, but in July it was reported in the newspapers that both were indisposed having succumbed to measles. The malady was to prove fatal, and the following passages are taken from an account of the Queen's death and lying in state. Six days later the King died.

After the body had been embalmed, it was placed in a leaden coffin, and laid upon tressels in the Governor's (Bogi's) bed-chamber. In a circle round the coffin are arranged the Royal war-cloaks, which are manufactured of feathers of various colours, and are used by the King and his Staff when in battle; on the lid, at the head of the coffin, is placed the Queen's Crown, it is a circle of yellow feathers. Several other circles,

158

composed of feathers of the same tint, are placed on the lid down to the foot. Several bunches of feathers, used by the Royal attendants to disperse the flies from her Majesty's person, are placed emblematically on the coffin lid. The principal one, used by Bogi, the Governor, stands with the handle on the ground at the head of the body, and the feather end drooping over the head of her Majesty. Two wax candles (lighted) are placed at the foot of the coffin, on a table covered with a white diaper.

The King passed a very good night, and yesterday morning said he had entertained a hope that he and his lamented consort would have been well enough to have been presented to the King of England on Wednesday next.

We are in the less grief for his Majesty's loss, as, we understand, he has four more wives at home.

The News, 11 July 1824

Maharajah Runjeet Singh *1780–1839*

Known as the 'Lion of the Punjab', Runjeet Singh was the last independent ruler of the Punjab. He could neither read nor write and was described in an obituary as 'selfish, sensual, and licentious in the extreme, regardless of all ties of affection, blood, or friendship, in the pursuit of ambition or pleasure'.

Proud, restless, ungovernable, impatient of restraint, he ruled with despotism over twenty millions of people, and aided by the fertile powers of his mighty genius, rose from a common thief to be a conqueror of princes, and became the friend and ally of the British Government in India.

The Annual Register of the year 1839

159

Prince Ernest Augustus, Duke of Cumberland
1771–1851

The Whig pamphleteers of the time had a field-day with this royal duke whose chief crimes were to be a High Tory and a violently anti-Catholic Protestant, as well as having undue influence (so the Whigs thought) over his brother, the Prince Regent. One pamphleteer went to prison for six months for the libellous accusation of murder. On his death *The Times* prefaced this obituary with the solemn indictment: 'The good which may be said of the royal dead is little or none – this succindecy [*sic*] has encapsulated the awful life of he who was surely the wickedest of Queen Victoria's wicked uncles.'

HRH Prince Ernest Augustus, Duke of Cumberland, was surely the most well loathed personage ever to have sprung from the illustrious head of our noble royal household of England. Amongst the crimes of which he was widely believed to be guilty were the foul murder of his valet, adultery with that valet's wife, sodomy, the blackmail of his illustrious brother, the Prince Regent, incest with his sister, and the indecent assault of the wife of the Lord Chamberlain, and plotting the assassination of his niece, Princess Victoria, heiress to the throne of England.

At the blessed moment in 1838 when Victoria succeeded to her rightful place, Prince Ernest became King of Hanover until his death. He ruled that place as a virtual autocrat, imprisoning all who dared to oppose him, but the Hanoverians bless his name to this day.

The Times, 20 November 1857

Napoleon III *1808–1873*

Nephew of Napoleon I, Louis Napoleon assumed headship of the Bonaparte family in 1832 and proclaimed himself Emperor of France in 1852. Deposed by the National Assembly at Bordeaux in 1871, he retired to England, to Chislehurst, where he died. Of his earlier stay in England *The Times* claimed complacently that 'he conceived for this country that quiet but steady attachment which seldom fails to spring up in the heart of those who spend a summer and winter among us. Among the French the Prince generally sought tools and accomplices; of the English he made friends and companions.' Admiring of his inexhaustible spirit of enterprise, the verdict was that

> With his unquestionable ability and some extraordinary gifts, it must be confessed he owed much to fortune. She repeatedly did wonderful things for him when his circumstances were critical. He came to count with too great confidence on her favours when they were showering down on him and he drew recklessly on his *prestige* instead of nursing it against gloomier days. It had been his aim to persuade his subjects that he was something more than mortal; when his mishaps proved his mortality, they resented the deception he had practised on them, and trampled their idol in the dust.
>
> *The Times*, 10 January 1873

161

Tewfik Pasha, Khedive of Egypt 1858–1892

Mohammed Tewfik became Khedive of Egypt in succession to his father, Ismail. On 26 June 1879, Ismail received a telegram from Constantinople informing him that he was deposed. Such was the nature of the event that by three o'clock that afternoon every one of his flatterers had deserted him and, while Tewfik was being proclaimed Khedive at the Citadel by a crowd which included officers who had sworn forty-eight hours before to die for Ismail, the deposed Khedive was playing backgammon with a solitary Englishman, apologizing for being unable to offer him coffee because he had no servants.

Tewfik had neither the great virtues nor the vices of his ancestors. Though well intentioned, he was inexperienced and had no authority over a dissatisfied people and disaffected army. Within five months of his accession, the British and French Governments stepped in and re-established the Dual Control to govern the country. Egypt was rescued from a state of administrative anarchy, but the Khedive was appointed by his allies to play a humiliating rôle in the affairs of his country.

> He was told to be obdurate, and he remained so until he found his head in chancery. He was then told to be conciliatory, and he distributed decorations. He was then, with fine humour, told to be dignified, and he was so until he was kicked, when he was exhorted to show a Christian spirit and forgive. When ultimatums came, supported with men-of-war, he was courageous. When the ultimatums were withdrawn and he was told that no men could be landed, he was less so. When soldiers did arrive he felt joyful until he learnt that their ammunition was at Cyprus, when he became sad. No man – outside of a British Cabinet – was ever placed in so humiliating or ridiculous a position.

The Times, 8 January 1892

Prince Alfred, Duke of Saxe-Coburg and Gotha 1844–1900

Queen Victoria's loyal and devoted subjects rightly judged her feelings on the death of her second son and fourth child which she recorded in her diary with the words, 'Oh God! my poor darling Alfie gone too . . . It is hard at eighty-one.' He died of cancer of the throat but as the symptoms first manifested themselves in 1898, it was not quite the 'sudden, unlooked for death' referred to here. Nor was he 'a stranger in England' since he had his own residence in Clarence House, where he spent several months of each year. However, distortion of the facts, for whatever reason, has long been regarded as the obituarist's prerogative.

Sudden in the real sense of the word, because generally unlooked for, the death of him whom we used to call our Sailor-Prince has affected all of us directly enough: much more for the sake of the Lady who loved him, the Queen who was his mother, the Empress who is beloved by so many millions. It is sixteen years since Her Majesty suffered so severe a blow as this; for it is sixteen years since the Duke of Albany died: and to-day the sympathy of everyone of us is with our Queen-Empress in her grief.

Called abroad by his duty, the Duke of Saxe-Coburg had for long been something of a stranger to us in England; but as Prince Alfred, and as the Duke of Edinburgh, he is not, nor can be, forgotten by any who knew him; while as a hard-working sailorman and an honest gentleman he was known to most of the Queen's millions of subjects. He loved his country and he loved the sea: as he showed when he declined the offer of the Crown of Greece. We know that his success in his profession was due to his own merits rather than to his exalted position; we know that he attained the high level of skill in seamanship that alone can justify the making of an Admiral; and we know that he was as much a man of practical worth as he was an accomplished artist. If of late years the Duke was found more inaccessible; if he failed to do with his Principality all that might have been done had he been called earlier to reign over it – that was due to the ill-health which overtook him, to be so greatly aggravated by the loss of his only son: whom now he has followed into the unseen world.

We dare not intrude into the privacy of a mother's grief; but it is ours to remember that it can be no small consolation to our Queen in her great loss to know that her son has left behind him a worthy record and an honourable memory.

Vanity Fair, July 1900

King Humbert I 1844–1900

Although the well-publicised simple life and homely ways of King Humbert, eldest son of Victor Emmanuel, won him the titles of *Il Re Citadino* and *il Padre del suo Populo*, they did not protect him from attempts against his life. Following two early assassination attempts, after the second of which he is reported as saying that they were one of 'the perquisites of his trade', he was finally killed at Monza. His assassin, Bressi, a Tuscan by birth and as much the subject of this obituary as his victim, was later discovered to have been chosen by lot to carry out the assassination, and he had returned from the United States expressly for this purpose.

The feeling of horror that has thrilled the civilised world with news of the assassination of so blameless a Sovereign as King Humbert must rouse the human – and, as some would call it, brutal – instinct of

164

revenge in many of us. The crime of Bressi makes one wonder whether he and his like ought to be treated as human beings, or as worse than the savage beast: for at least the killing of the latter is natural and has reason. Bressi's act is unnatural and wholly unreasonable: unless indeed it were done in that spirit of self-glorification which finds satisfaction in notoriety of any kind. And if such a crime as Bressi's can be committed for so poor and so vain a reason as that, it becomes questionable whether the only way to deal with such a criminal is not to make him suffer something worse than what we, in our civilisation, call 'the extreme penalty of death': not indeed to punish him, but to make harder, by the example of his suffering, the growing repetition of the most horrible and most unreasoning crime of these latter days.

We say so much with full sense of responsibility. Here is a vile miscreant who in any case cannot be held fit to live. Here is a crime that has robbed the world of a noble King, whose worst fault was his amiability to his people: a crime which has overwhelmed with sudden killing grief a Sovereign Lady who has most greatly loved her subjects, of whom her husband's murderer is one; a crime which has rolled a mighty wave of dismayed sorrow across a whole Continent: yet the vain assassin cares for none of these things, since he has glorified himself by making the world ring with his execrated name. It may be that he will suffer in the calmer moments of his imprisonment. It may be that he will suffer horribly. But the material of which he is made will not know this. Those others of his kind see him affect a brave glorying in his terrible act when he is on trial; they see the self-styled hero who, for notoriety's sake, poses as a martyr: and the sight has influence on the mindlessness of those who are made of the same silly stuff.

165

There are but few such, no doubt: but the rest of us have to remember when considering this kind that all the chain of loyalty is in this matter no stronger than its weakest link.

Would it not be well, then, to let those persons of whom assassins are made see the other side of the picture? In some countries – which we in our superior knowledge call barbarous – such a man as Bressi would be sure to suffer: and his suffering would cure some like him, and encourage others not to be like him. Nihilism is dead in Russia; but the Bressi crime is repeated in the rest of Europe. The best of Sovereigns is threatened. Our own Prince of Wales has been shot at, and civilised Belgium by its treatment of Sipido did nothing if it did not encourage Bressi to commit the crime at which the world is shuddering to-day.

Vanity Fair, July 1900

Queen Victoria 1819–1901

Queen Victoria's death was marked by universal mourning but also a certain alarm, as, while she lived, England's power seemed indisputable. 'Oh! Dearest George,' wrote the Queen's first cousin, Augusta of Strelitz, to the Duke of Cambridge, 'What a calamity! . . . anxiety terrible as to what poor England will have to go through *now!* God have mercy on us all!' *The Times* declared that people felt they had lost not only a Sovereign whom they had almost come to 'worship', but 'a personal benefactress'.

At half-past six on Tuesday evening in last week – just after we had gone to press – died at Osborne the greatest Queen that the world has seen. So much is felt, without words, by many millions; and when the

166

historian shall come, with better light than ours, to appreciate the influence upon the world of Queen Victoria, he must record the true fact that never before in the story of the ages has any Woman exerted so great a sway over so many millions for so long a time with so entire an influence for good. And the millions have appreciated this. There is not a subject of the King living that has not to repress a sob when he remembers that he has heard the hymn 'God Save the Queen' for the last time. For there is scarce a man in the Empire that the world has yet seen – who has not thought of Queen Victoria as something like a Mother.

It is not less curious than true; and when we wonder at it we are amazed to think that we can scarce know why we venerated the Queen as we did. The very sight of that little Lady in black as she drove through the Park, and rather sadly, yet most sweetly, smiled at her humbler subjects as they gave her welcome among them, made us feel her influence in a way that was unexpected before. Her Majesty was full of virtue; she had many qualities; she was known as an earnest worker for her country. But there was something more than all this. Probably no great race ever felt more loyal than her subjects felt towards Queen Victoria. Was not this because for sixty years and more the knowledge of her own loyalty to her people had forced itself upon them? Never, surely was Sovereign more loyal. Let any who doubts turn back and read a few of those beautiful, simple, yet exquisitely-worded messages that have been received from the Queen by those who have suffered, and have been treasured as beyond price. From that affection-ate message 'From a Widow to a Widow' to the last kind words that were sent to a dead soldier's wife, there is none that has not marked the loyal sympathy of the Woman and the Queen who is taken from us. If

167

there be any truth at all in the old Roman saying, 'Vox populi, vox Dei,' has that truth ever been more fully appreciated than it was by the Queen who loved her people so well; the Queen who had a kind word for the poorest of us in distress; the Queen who had a tear for every soldier who fell fighting for her?

And it is not only in the kindness of sympathy that Her Majesty shone so clearly. Good words, they say, are worth much and cost little. Queen Victoria's good words were the least part of what she did for her people. She devoted her life to her country. Her sense of duty never wavered; her clearness of judgement never failed; her earnest work has never been known in all its fulness. True in everything, brave at all times, full of faith in God and her people, never sparing herself in their cause, she made herself venerated by a race that is not given by Nature to veneration. Her influence has been beyond measure for years past. It is not at an end now.

Vanity Fair, January 1901

The following obituary which was written at the time of Queen Victoria's death by the English poet and traveller, Wilfrid Scawen Blunt, and published in *My Diaries* is in marked contrast. The language was somewhat modified and the last sentence deleted on publication.

As to Her Majesty personally, one does not like to say all one thinks, even in one's journal. By all I have heard of her, she was in her old age a dignified but commonplace old soul and bourgeois, like many of our dowagers. Privately all lovers of liberty will rejoice at the end of a bloody and abominable reign.

Wilfrid Scawen Blunt, *My Diaries* (1919, 1920)

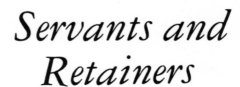

Servants and
Retainers

Living? The servants will do that for us.

Axël by Auguste Villiers de l'Isle-Adam
(1838–1889)

Henry Garman *died 1729*

Last Thursday Night, the Coroner's Inquest sate upon the Body of Henry Garman, Butler to the Temple-Hall, who hang'd himself on Tuesday, last, and brought in their verdict Lunacy: By the evidence it appear'd that the first Time he discover'd a Disorder in his senses, was upon the Death of his Grandfather, who dy'd a little while since; but more remarkably on Sunday last, when a Country clergyman preach'd at the Temple-Church from these words, 'What doth it profit a man if he gains the whole world and loseth his own soul.' In the middle of the sermon, as the Minister was preaching, he started up and said to this effect: 'Oh! Mr. Parson, This Doctrine may do well enough in the country, but not here among the lawyers.'

St. James Evening Post, September 1729

Henry Wanyford *died 1741*

Mr. Henry Wanyford, late Steward to the Earl of Essex. He was of so large a size, that the top of the Herse was obliged to be taken off before the Coffin could be admitted, and so heavy, that they were forced to move it along the Church-yard upon Rollers.

The Gentleman's Magazine, December 1741

Anthony Mascarenhas *died 1783*

At Lisbon, a negro, named Anthony Mascarenhas, aged 110. Born at Mandinga in Africa, he had been a slave to Counsellor Don Joseph Mascarenhas Pacheco, with whom, like a faithful servant, he had remained 18 years in prison.

The Gentleman's Magazine, June 1783

Cooba *1681–1791*

In St. Elizabeth's, aged 110, an old Negro woman, named Cooba. She belonged to the Hon. Thomas Chambers, esq. custos of that parish. From her master, and a numerous family of descendents, down to the fourth generation, she had every comfort and convenience of life; besides which, having been entirely at liberty to do as she pleased for 20 or 30 years past, she used regularly to visit a circle of acquaintance for many miles around, and not only was well received both by whites and blacks, but made herself useful to them, as she possessed her recollection to the last, and had her senses so perfectly, that, to instance only her sight, which generally fails first, she could see to thread a needle, and was still so active, that, a few months before her death, she was seen to dance with as much apparent ease as a girl of 15 years of age.

The Gentleman's Magazine, October 1791

Mr Robertson 1656–1793

At Hopetoun-hall, near Edinburgh, at the surprising age of 137, a man of the name of Robertson. This modern patriarch had always lived in the family of the lords of that place, whom he served in the capacity of inspector of the lead works for four complete generations, besides the time elapsed since the birth of the present possessor, thereby expressing the zeal and fidelity of an old and worthy servant, during the space of 110 years.

The Gentleman's Magazine, June 1793

Thomas Pope *died 1832*

At Old Windsor, aged 96, Thomas Pope, who had followed the employment of a shepherd, with little exception, from the age when he received two pence per day. He was an example to others in the humble station of life in which he was placed, having brought up a large family without parochial aid. His known good character procured him many friends, who supplied every want his advanced age required. At his particular wish, his crook and bell were buried with him – the crook in one hand, and the bell in the other. He was followed to the grave by his family, and his master paid the last mark of respect to so faithful a servant.

The Gentleman's Magazine, September 1832

John Brown *1826–1883*

The inscription chosen by Queen Victoria for the headstone of John Brown's tomb reads, 'The devoted and faithful personal attendant of Queen Victoria'. That, and the following obituary in *The Times* which the Queen assisted in composing, understate the attachment between a Balmoral gillie and his sovereign as witnessed by her scandalized family and the world at large.

COURT CIRCULAR
Windsor Castle, March 28

We have to record the death of Mr. John Brown, the Queen's personal attendant, which took place at Windsor Castle at a quarter past 11 o'clock on Tuesday evening, the 27th instant, of erysipelas. This melancholy event has caused the deepest regret to the Queen, the Royal Family, and all the members of the Royal household. To Her Majesty the loss is irreparable, and the death of this truly faithful and devoted servant has been a grievous shock to the Queen. In 1849, Mr. John Brown entered the Queen's service as one of the Balmoral gillies, and by his careful attention, steadiness, and intelligence he rose in 1858 to the position of the Queen's personal servant in Scotland, which, in 1864, was extended to that of constant personal attendant on Her Majesty on all occasions. During the last 18 years and a half, he served Her Majesty constantly and never once absented himself from his duty for a single day. He has accompanied the Queen in her daily walks and drives, and all her journeys and expeditions, as well as personally waiting on her at banquets, &c. An honest, faithful, and devoted follower, a trustworthy, discreet, and straightforward man, and possessed of strong sense, he filled a position of great and anxious responsibility, the duties of which he performed with such constant and unceasing care as to secure for himself the real friendship of the Queen.

173   *The Times*, 29 March 1883

Soldiers and Sailors

They shall not grow old, as we that are left grow old:
Age shall not weary them, nor the years condemn.
At the going down of the sun and in the morning
We will remember them.

Poems for the Fallen by Laurence Binyon
(1869–1943)

Christiana Davis *died 1739*

Mrs. Christiana Davis, who for several years served as
a dragoon, and behaved with great resolution in
many engagements.

The Scots Magazine, July 1739

George Dundas of Dundas *1752–1792*

A hero's death for George Dundas, a ship's mate and a member of the
twenty-third generation of a remarkable Scottish family who 'yielded
to none', according to a contemporary account, 'whether regarded in
point of antiquity, or of the number of conspicuous individuals its
different branches have produced'.

George Dundas, of Dundas, esq. commander of the
Winterton East Indiaman, unfortunately perished in
the wreck of that vessel, near Madagascar, a victim to
his humanity and attention to the passengers, not one
of whom was lost, the three ladies that died having
suffered through fatigue after getting to land. Mr. D.
the chief of that ancient and distinguished family,
only son of James D. of D. M.P. for Linlithgowshire,
by Jane, daughter of William, 13th Lord Forbes, was
born at Thoulouse in France, while his parents were
on their travels abroad. On his last voyage home from
India, his vessel was reckoned in such imminent
danger, that the stoutest and most experienced seamen, officers and all, threw themselves down on the
deck in despair. Mr. D. was the only person unappal-
led at the approach of death; and his example and

exhortations operated so forcibly as to rouse the men to exert themselves in so vigorous a manner, that the ship was saved and brought into Plymouth. Of 264 passengers, soldiers, and seamen, no less than 222 got safe to land, while the gallant commander, and his first mate, with a degree of inattention to themselves, of which the present days furnish few examples, fell victims to their humanity.

The Gentleman's Magazine, August, 1792

Captain Norton and Mr Phythian died 1794

In St. Croix, Captain Norton, of the ship, Christopher, and also Mr. Phythian, his carpenter. These two very deserving and steady officers, having the misfortune to lose their vessel, which accidentally got on her anchor and bilged, the loss so affected their spirits as to bring on a fever, which carried them off in a few days.

The Gentleman's Magazine, June 1794

Horatio, Viscount Nelson 1758–1805

Lord Nelson expired with the words, 'Thank God, I have done my duty' on his lips. His body was brought back to England in his flagship *Victory,* and after lying in state in the Painted Hall at Greenwich was buried in the crypt of St Paul's Cathedral. The great service he rendered to his country was commemorated by the column surmounted by a statue of him in Trafalgar Square, and by an abundance of mediocre verse. The following passage perhaps summarizes the admiration of most of his contemporaries.

In tracing this illustrious mariner, from the ardour of his boyish days to the active magnanimity with which he closed his glorious life, the mind must be dazzled with the brilliant variety of his actions in every part of it. What danger has he not encountered? What hardship has he not suffered? What obstacle has he not subdued? What climate has he not endured? What seas has he not sailed? What service has he not performed? What service has he left undone? – When it was his rank to obey, he had the confidence of his Commanders: when he was advanced to command, he had the enthusiasm of those who obeyed him. The same promptitude of thought and resource, the same rapid movement, the same application of the best possible means to the ends he had in view, whether at the instant or in expectation, seemed equally to operate in his mind, and to animate his genius in every situation, and all the extraordinary emergencies, of his professional life.

The Times, 14 November 1805

Mrs Bayne *died 1805*

During the funeral procession of Lord Nelson's remains on the river, a lady of the name of Bayne, related to the late Capt. William Bayne, who lost his life in the West Indies under Lord Rodney, was so affected at the scene, that she fell into hysterics, and died in a few minutes.

The Gentleman's Magazine, January 1806

Mary Ralphson *1698–1808*

Lately, aged 110 years and six months, Mary Ralphson, of Kent-Street, Liverpool; she married R. Ralphson, a private under Duke William, and was an attendant on her husband in several engagements. In the Battle of Dettingen, during the heart of the conflict, she observed a dragoon fall by her side; she disguised herself in his clothes, mounted his charger, and regained the retreating army, found her husband, returned to England, and accompanied him in his later campaigns with Duke William.

The Examiner, July 1808

Major-General John Murray *died 1832*

In the American War of Independence Murray, with a small body of troops, captured Fort Niagara. This 'brilliant affair' did much to compensate for a rather inauspicious start to his military career.

He entered the army in 1793, as Ensign in the 37th regiment, which he accompanied in the following year to Ostend; where, in one of the early sorties, he was wounded in the face by a ball, which remained in his head for more than a fortnight, and then fell through the roof of his mouth. After having obtained his Lieutenancy in the same regiment, he was taken prisoner, with nearly half of his corps, on the banks of the Waal in Holland, in consequence of mistaking, from their dress, a division of the French cavalry for the British.

The Gentleman's Magazine, May 1832

Captain Hesse *died 1832*

At Nogent, near Paris, Capt. Hesse, an Aid-de-Camp of the Duke of Wellington, in a duel at the Bois de Vincennes, by Comte Leon, a natural son of the Emperor Napoleon, in consequence of some disputes which took place at a card party. Mr. Hesse had for his seconds the Count d'Esterno, a German, and an English officer; and the seconds of Count Leon were Colonel Fournier and M. May, another French officer. General Gourgaud and the Surgeon Major of the 11th of Artillery, in garrison at Vincennes, were also present. Scarcely were they placed at the distance agreed upon, when the adversaries advanced five paces towards each other. Mr. Hesse fired first, without waiting, and immediately Count Leon fired in his turn, and wounded Mr. Hesse in the chest. M. Leon, on a journey to Rome last year, was received most affectionately by the family of Buonaparte. Queen Hortensia made him a present of a button, recommending him to wear it under any circumstances were [sic] he might incur danger, and adding, that it would be fortunate for him. M. Leon wore it, for the first time, on his breast on the above occasion.

The Gentleman's Magazine, April 1832

Admiral Williams-Freeman 1742–1832

In 1780 Captain Williams (who changed his name to Williams-Freeman in 1821 and attained the rank of admiral of the fleet three days after the accession of William IV) was appointed to the frigate *Flora.* Off Ushant he engaged a French ship, *La Nymphe,* and for an hour a gallant action was fought with equal bravery on both sides. When the *Flora*'s wheel was shot away, the French tried to board, but they were repulsed by the English, and driven back to their own ship. The *Flora*'s seamen pursued them sword in hand, cut down their colours and carried *La Nymphe* by storm.

A magnificent crucifix, with a certificate under the Pope's hand that it was formed of a part of the cross on which Christ suffered, incased in silver, form a trophy of this victory, now in possession of the victor's family. It was found on board the Flora when the battle was over, and undoubtedly had been thrown there from la Nymphe to stimulate the ardor of the French sailors on boarding.

The Gentleman's Magazine, April 1832

Lieutenant-General Theophilus Lewis
1753–1832

Colonel Commandant in the Royal Marines, during the course of a long career in the defence of his country Lewis had been present in ten general actions at sea.

The death of this aged veteran was occasioned by an altercation and scuffle which he had with his drunken housekeeper, of whose violence he had been frequently warned by his friends; but whom, being an old servant, he could never be prevailed upon to discharge.

At an inquest held on his body, his grandson, Theophilus Lewis, a boy about fourteen years of age, deposed that at about 20 minutes before eight o'clock on the preceding evening he had heard a noise as if two persons were squabbling in the passage; he proceeded to the spot and found his grandfather lying on his housekeeper, Ann McCarthy, at the bottom of the stairs. The deceased then got up, and said that Ann had bitten him, and went into the parlour. Ann then went to shut the street door, but was prevented by persons outside. Deceased followed her along the passage, when another squabble took place. He then returned to the parlour with a steady step, but immediately upon entering fell backward with his head outside the door. The witness believed that there was no blow given to cause the fall. He was placed between two chairs, and did not show the least signs of life.

The Jury, after a short deliberation, returned a verdict of 'Died by the visitation of God, of apoplexy, produced by excitement'.

The Gentleman's Magazine, March 1833

Admiral Sir Thomas Foley 1757–1833

Foley was flag captain on the *Elephant* in support of Nelson at the Battle of Copenhagen. When Sir Hyde Parker, who was commanding the fleet, gave the signal to discontinue the action,

Nelson betrayed great emotion, and it was to Capt. Foley that he exclaimed, in that mood of mind which sports with bitterness, 'Leave off the action! Now, d – n me if I do. You know Foley, I have only one eye, and have a right to be blind sometimes;' and then, putting the glass to his blind eye, observed, 'I really do not see the signal.'

The Gentleman's Magazine, March 1833

Henry William Paget, Marquess of Anglesey 1768–1854

Referred to by his descendants as 'one leg' or the Waterloo Marquess, Lord Anglesey was the Iron Duke's second-in-command at that memorable battle. When surrounded on his death bed by his family, it is said that his last words were, 'What brigade is on duty?' When answered that it was not his own, nor was he neglecting his duty, he was then ready to die.

> Since the soldier's drawn sword first glittered in the sunshine, never did a more fearless or chivalrous officer support the honour of his country. Lord Anglesey belonged to a race of nobles who have passed away from us; he was the last of the race, and we shall know them no more. Your modern English peer is a sharp land agent or conveyancer, or a jocular, hair-splitting law lord, or if he be of a younger generation, he is a painful devourer of blue-books. A man ready to talk for about three hours on the condition of Central Asia, or the statistics of dandelions in Salop, but a nobleman he is not, in the sense in which Lord Anglesey was one. Society may possibly have gained by the change – we simply notify the fact that a genus is extinct, of which Lord Anglesey was a brilliant example.
>
> *The Times,* 3 February 1854

General Garibaldi 1807–1882

The Italian people admired above all else 'an example of disinterested patriotism and of reckless bravery' it was said, and this they found in the character of Garibaldi. He had the ideal lion nature in him, according to *The Times*, 'all the dignity and gentleness, the sudden flash of anger, the forgiveness, the absence of all rancour, malice, or uncharitableness'. He was lion-like in appearance, too, with a mass of tawny hair and a full red beard.

His gigantic popularity stretched from Italy, where he was one of the great patriotic heroes of the nineteenth century, to London, 'where, in 1864, he fairly ran away from the fine ladies who seemed at a loss to know how a true lion should be lionised'.

> Garibaldi's exploits were well qualified to excite popular admiration, and there was something both imposing and winning in his personal character. His picturesque appearance was in itself an element of popularity, and his extravagant utterances caused him to be regarded as a representative of the democracy. The excitement which attended his visit to England eighteen years ago is not forgotten. The streets of London were impassable on the day on which he was expected to take up his quarters in a ducal palace; and it was observed that the multitude consisted almost entirely of the poorer classes. His keen enjoyment of his reception produced on his part a friendly feeling to England which was never afterwards disavowed. He showed no resentment when the Government of the day deprived him of the pleasure of a provincial tour which was thought likely to cause disturbance and embarrassment. The persuasive eloquence of Mr. Gladstone was employed first to hasten his departure from England, and then to assure Parliament that the heroic guest had shortened his visit of his own accord.

The Saturday Review, 10 June 1882

General Gordon *1833–1885*

In 1883 'Chinese Gordon' — so named because of his distinguished career in China — accepted an invitation from the King of the Belgians to undertake important duties in the Congo. The British Government refused to sanction the posting and he was preparing to renounce his commission in the Army when he was summoned by the British Cabinet. Britain had withdrawn support for the Khedive in resisting the overrunning of the Sudan by the Mahdi and Gordon was asked to proceed to Khartoum to effect the withdrawal of the garrisons and evacuate the Egyptian and European population. He was persuaded by popular opinion to accept. On 26 January 1885, before the relief expedition, which the British Government had been dilatory in sending, could reach him, Gordon was betrayed and in the general massacre that ensued he was killed. Khartoum fell to the Mahdi after a gallant siege of 317 days.

> There can be little doubt that General Gordon in accepting the mission to Khartoum was actuated by only two considerations — first, a sense of duty; and, secondly, a belief that if he could not do the greatest possible good he might still do much that would benefit the people and promote the chances of peace. His mode of reasoning was simple. It ran thus: 'If God wills it, nothing is impossible. He has placed this work before me, and it is my part only to obey. At the worst I die or am killed, which is nothing, and nobody else is involved.'
>
> *The Times,* 12 February 1885

John Paulet, Marquess of Winchester
1801–1887

Premier marquess of England and Hereditary Bearer of the Cup of Maintenance, he and his immediate forebears were well connected at Court and the Prince Regent was a frequent guest at Amport, the family seat in Hampshire. As a young man he owed his commission in the army to the royal visitor's predilection for the house Jamaica rum.

The Regent, whenever he visited Amport, was given some of this rum, and he appreciated it so much that he was in the habit of taking two bottles away with him when he left. On this occasion, however, the servant forgot to place the two bottles in the Regent's travelling carriage, and the error having been discovered a short time after the Royal party had left, Lord Winchester, then Lord Wiltshire, was sent off by his father on horseback to overtake the Regent's carriage and hand him the two bottles of rum. When he overtook the party the Regent complimented him on his horsemanship, and promised him a commission in his own regiment, the 10th Hussars.

The Annual Register of the year 1887

Rupert Brooke 1887–1915

On 26 April 1915, *The Times* published an unsigned obituary of a few lines. Written by Edward Marsh, it ended, 'He died before he had fulfilled his own hopes or ours; but either we believe in waste altogether or not at all. And if any seeming waste is not waste, there is none in a young life full of promise and joyfully laid down.' Marsh's few sentences were only a preface to a valediction published over the initials of the First Lord of the Admiralty. Written at a critical moment in the operations, when the first reports of the Gallipoli landing were hourly expected, the generosity of spirit informing every line anticipates the idolatry which was shortly to be lavished on Brooke's memory.

> Rupert Brooke is dead. A telegram from the Admiralty at Lemnos tells us that this life has closed at the moment when it seemed to have reached its springtime. A Voice had become audible, a note had been struck, more true, more thrilling, more able to do justice to the nobility of our youth in arms engaged in this present war, than any other – more able to express their thoughts of self-surrender, and with a power to carry comfort to those who watched them so intently from afar. The voice has been swiftly stilled. Only the echoes and the memory remain; but they will linger.
>
> During the last few months of his life, months of preparation in gallant comradeship and open air, the poet-soldier told with all the simple force of genius the sorrow of youth about to die, and the sure triumphant consolations of a sincere and valiant spirit. He expected to die for the dear England whose beauty and majesty he knew; and he advanced towards the brink in perfect serenity, with absolute conviction of the rightness of his country's cause, and a heart devoid of hate for fellow-men.
>
> The thoughts to which he gave expression in the

very few incomparable war sonnets which he has left behind will be shared by many thousands of young men moving resolutely and blithely forward into this, the hardest, the cruellest, and the least-rewarded of all the wars that men have fought. They are a whole history and revelation of Rupert Brooke himself. Joyous, fearless, versatile, deeply instructed, with classic symmetry of mind and body, he was all that one would wish England's noblest sons to be in days when no sacrifice but the most precious is acceptable, and the most precious is that which is most freely proffered.

The Times, 29 April 1915

The courage and honest dedication of those involved in the First World War is keenly apparent both in the content and in the boyish jargon of these two obituaries of unknown soldiers. They serve to remind us that for every Rupert Brooke, ten thousand ordinary soldiers were killed and *forgotten*.

2nd Lt. Edgehill *died 1918*

Second Lieutenant Ashley Gay Edghill, Lancashire Fuseliers, attached T. M. B. who died on April 15 of wounds received the day before, was the only child of Mr. and Mrs. Gay Edghill, of Applethwaites, Barbados and grandson of the late Dr. W. Jackson Cummins of Cork. He received his commission in September 1916, and went to the front in December of the same year. The chaplain of his battalion writes:— 'Through his death we have lost one of the best and straightest officers we have ever had, and one who was popular with both officers and men in the very best sense of the word. I have rarely, if ever, known a more painstaking and conscientious officer, and it is certain his men have never had a better friend. The world has been a better place for his having been in it.'

The Times, 28 April 1918

2nd Lt. *Reading* died 1918

Second Lieutenant J. Reading, R. T. C., reported missing on March 26, is now unofficially reported to have been killed, aged 22. He was the only son of Mr. A. Y. Reading, Knodishall Lodge, Suffolk and was educated at Woodbridge Grammar School. His Commanding Officer writes:— 'I cannot say how much I miss him as a member of the squadron. He was a charming boy; and a very gallant one, too. During the great offensive he did good work, brought back reports of the highest value, bombed and machine-gunned enemy troops in a way that one could not but feel the greatest admiration and courage, and I regarded him as one of the most promising pilots in the squadron. Apart from being his Commanding Officer, I liked him as a friend, and the feeling was shared by the whole squadron. He was always so cheery and bright.'

The Times, 28 April 1918

Sudden Deaths

The World's a bubble; and the life of man
Less than a span.

The World by Francis Bacon (1561–1626)

Mrs Fitzherbert *died 1782*

Mrs. Fitzherbert, relict of the late rev. Mr. F. of Northamptonshire. On the Wednesday evening before her death this lady went to Drury-Lane theatre, in company with some friends, to see the Beggar's Opera. On Mr. Bannister's making his appearance in the character of Polly, the whole audience were thrown into an uproar of laughter; unfortunately the actor's whimsical appearance had a fatal effect on Mrs. Fitzherbert; she could not suppress the laugh that seized her on the first view of this enormous representation; and before the second act was over she was obliged to leave the theatre. Mrs. F. not being able to banish the figure from her memory, was thrown into hysterics, which continued without intermission until Friday morning, when she expired.

The Gentleman's Magazine, April 1782

William Marsh *died 1782*

In Newgate, Wm. Marsh, who, with three other lads, was convicted in May session, 1781, of robbing Wm. Wilson, on the highway, on Salt-petre-bank, and respited during his Majesty's pleasure. His death was occasioned by the following accident: On Saturday the deceased, and several of the prisoners, being in a frolicksome humour, had procured soot, red ochre, &c. and with it daubed the faces of several of their fellow-prisoners, one of whom at the time acting as hair-dresser to one of the prisoners, having in his hand a pair of sharp concave tongs, irritated by the smart in his eyes occasioned by the soot, threw the tongs promiscuously amongst them, which entered several inches into Marsh's forehead, of which he languished till Tuesday.

The Gentleman's Magazine, June 1782

John Burton *died* 1793

At Wirksworth, Mr. John Burton, baker. His wife who was pregnant of her seventh child was so agitated when she heard the doleful sound of the passing bell, that she miscarried; and, on the evening of the 4th, whilst the bell was tolling for the funeral of her departed husband, she expired.

The Gentleman's Magazine, May 1793

Mr Houghton *died* 1806

Mr. Houghton, shoemaker, in the Butter-market at Bury St. Edmund's. He was in apparent good health, chopping a faggot, the same afternoon, when he accidentally cut one of his fingers, and, on his wife's expressing a wish to dress it, he said, 'Never mind, my dear; what is this wound compared to Lord Nelson's?' and immediately fell down in an apoplectic fit, from which he never recovered to utter another sentence.

The Gentleman's Magazine, January 1806

Anna Maria de Mendoza Rios
died 1817

At Reigate, Anna Maria, widow of the late Josef de
Mendoza Rios, esq. a gentleman distinguished for
his arithmetical calculations, and officially employed
upon a most important discovery in bringing the
longitude to a fixed and invariable point. The error of
one figure in some millions of numbers so completely
disconcerted his mind, that in a fit of intellectual
despondency, he retired to his chamber, and hung
himself.

The Gentleman's Magazine, August 1817

Giuseppe Naldi 1770–1820

This account of the Italian singer's death, 'occasioned by the bursting
of a new-invented self-acting cooking apparatus', was extracted from
the *Moniteur*.

This celebrated buffo-performer, having been invited
to dine with N. Garcia, immediately on his arrival
with his wife and daughter, proceeded to examine the
accelerated process of cooking by the self-acting boiler (*la marmite autoclave*). By an imprudent and fatal
inadvertency, M. Naldi, with the tongs, stopped the
valve, and the compression increased the heat to such
a degree, that an explosion ensued; the lid of the
boiler came in contact with his forehead, completely
severed the skull, and stretched him dead at the feet
of his daughter.

The Annual Register of the year 1820

A *Showman* died 1827

The keeper of a caravan of wild beasts in Bedminster being in want of an attendant, a person, who had from his infancy been accustomed to the business, offered his services, and was accepted. He was cautioned not to go within the reach of any of the beasts; this caution, however, he unhappily neglected. A party came to see the animals, and, as the lion was asleep, and did not appear willing to rise, the man imprudently went into his den. The beast suddenly awoke, and darted forward one of his paws, with which he seized the showman by the shoulder, and, at the same moment, with the other he dreadfully lacerated the face. The man cried piteously, and struggled to get loose, but his efforts were in vain, and the lion, now infuriated, seized him by the throat with his mouth, and held him in that situation till death put a period to his sufferings. A gentleman happening to pass who lived in the neighbourhood, immediately brought his pistols, and another person called to a blacksmith, who had a piece of iron red hot, to afford assistance, but it was twenty minutes before the animal would quit his prey, although his mouth was much burned; at length the head of the man fell from his jaws, and the body was drawn from the cage. Under ordinary circumstances the animal was exceedingly quiet and docile.

The Annual Register of the year 1827

Mary Ann Collins 1861–1877

Mary Ann Collins, aged sixteen years, employed at
the Valley Paper Mill in Verona Pa., has just met a
shocking death. Starting to answer a call, she walked
into a hatchway, which was obscured by steam aris-
ing from a vat of boiling water and vitriol. She was
precipitated directly into the vat and must have died
very speedily. In three minutes after she fell her body
was taken out, scalded white.

The Washington Post, 27 December 1877

Comte de Chambord 1820–1883

Bourbon claimant to the French throne, the Comte de Chambord twice had the opportunity of declaring himself king, but, in the opinion of *The Times*, 'was deficient in personal courage' and never stretched out his hand for the crown. He created, by his feebleness, confusion which 'darkened the political waters like the discharges of an ink-fish'.

His obituary included the following description of the death of his father, the Duc de Berry, assassinated under the portico of the Old Opera House in Paris in 1820. As he escorted the Duchesse de Berry to her coach, humming a snatch from Gluck's *Orphée*, he was stabbed in the back with such violence that the knife penetrated right through his chest and pierced the blue moiré Riband of the Order of the Holy Spirit which he was wearing.

> The scene of the Prince's final hour was dramatic beyond description. He was carried into the private *foyer* of the Opera, and there, mingling with singers in their paint and ballet-dancers in their tinsel, were presently gathered all the members of the royal family, the Ministers, the great officers of State. The King arrived from the Tuileries – old Louis XVIII., impotent in his feet, and hobbling painfully along, with his black gaiters, starched cravat, and powdered hair, which made him look like an old-fashioned notary. The Comte d'Artois was there too, his handsome face, usually so serene, pinched with anguish; and so was the portly Duc d'Orléans – afterwards Louis Philippe – who had a difficult part to play under the malevolent glances of courtiers seeking in his physiognomy for some sign of satisfaction at an event which appeared likely to establish the fortunes of his family. When all the illustrious company were assembled round the 'property' mattress on which the Duke lay dying, the mild and polished Duc de Quelen, Archbishop of Paris – the last of the *grand*

seigneur prelates, who wore diamonds and rubies like a Court beauty – walked in bearing the viaticum and attended by choristers with incense. He was preceded by a vicar-general, who scattered holy water around him with an asperges brush to purify the place; and, indeed, the Archbishop's first care was to consecrate the room, in consequence of which the building was never more used as an opera-house after that day.

The Times, 25 August 1883

Theatricals

Our revels now are ended. These our actors,
As I foretold you, were all spirits and
Are melted into air, into thin air:
And, like the baseless fabric of this vision,
The cloud-capp'd towers, the gorgeous palaces,
The solemn temples, the great globe itself,
Yea, all which it inherit, shall dissolve
And, like this insubstantial pageant faded,
Leave not a rack behind. We are such stuff
As dreams are made on, and our little life
Is rounded with a sleep.

The Tempest by William Shakespeare
(1564–1616)

David Garrick *1716–1779*

Garrick was a man of many careers – a magnificent actor, an accomplished dramatist, an exceptional theatrical producer and director and a respected critic. His death was marked by Dr Johnson's famous words which Mrs Garrick had engraved on her husband's monument in Lichfield Cathedral: 'I am disappointed by that stroke of death, which has eclipsed the gaiety of nations, and impoverished the public stock of harmless pleasure.'

Having at school performed the part of Sergeant Kite with applause, Mr. Garrick engaged with Mr. Gifford, at the theatre in Goodman Fields in 1744. The character he then attempted was that of Richard the Third; and he performed it in a manner which fixed his reputation on that basis upon which it stood, as the first actor of the times, during the rest of his life. Two circumstances were observed on his first night's performance; one, that, on his entrance on the stage, he was under so much embarrassment that for some time he was unable to speak; the other, that, having exerted himself with much vehemence in the first two acts, he became so hoarse as to be almost incapable of finishing the character. This difficulty was obviated by a person behind the scenes recommending him to take the juice of a seville orange which he fortunately had in his pocket.

It would be impossible to enumerate the several small pieces of poetry which Mr. Garrick used to throw out from time to time to compliment his friends, or to celebrate public occasions. We shall, however, just mention here that in 1759 Dr. Hill wrote a pamphlet, inituted [*sic*], 'To D. Garrick, Esq; the Petition of I, in behalf of herself and her sisters.' The purport of it was to charge Mr. Garrick with mispronouncing some words including the letter I, as *furm* for firm, *vurtue* for virtue, and others.

The pamphlet is now forgotten; but the following Epigram, which Mr. Garrick wrote on the occasion, deserves to be preserved, as one of the best in the English language.

To Dr. Hill, upon his petition of the letter I to David Garrick, Esq.

If 'tis true, as you say, that I've injur'd a letter,
I'll change my notes soon, and I hope for the better;
May the just right of letters, as well as of men,
Hereafter be fix'd by the tongue and the pen!
Most devoutly I wish that they both have their due,
And that I may never be mistaken for U.

In 1766 Mr. Garrick wrote in concert with Mr. Colman the excellent comedy of *The Clandestine Marriage* in which the death of Mr. Quinn was very pathetically taken notice of in the prologue. Mr. Quinn was the only performer of any reputation when Mr. Garrick first appeared on the stage, and he had likewise been one of his earliest composers. When he saw the success which attended the performance of his rival, he observed with his usual spleen that 'Garrick was a new religion. Whitfield was followed for a time, but they would all come to church again.' Mr. Garrick replied as follows:

Pope Quinn, who damns all churches but his own,
Complains 'that *Heresy* corrupts the town,
That *Whitfield Garrick* has misled the age,
And taints the sound religion of the stage;
Schism, he cries, has turn'd the nation's brain,
But eyes will open, and to *church* again.'
Thou great infallible! forebear to roar,
Thy bulls and errors are rever'd no more;
When doctrines meet with general approbation,
It is not *Heresy,* but *Reformation.*

201

Mr. Garrick died at the age of 63 years leaving behind him the character of a friendly, humane, charitable, and (notwithstanding many idle reports we may add) liberal man; one who felt for distress, relieved it; a cheerful companion, a pleasing writer, and the first actor of this or any other age.

The Gentleman's Magazine, June 1779

Madame Rollan 1713–1788

Professional rivalry has long been an occupational hazard of the stage.

Lately, at London, in her 75th year, Madame Rollan. She was a principal dancer on Covent Garden stage, so far back as 54 years ago, and following that profession, by private teaching, to the last year of her life. She had so much celebrity in her day, that having one evening sprained her ankle, no less an actor that Quin was ordered by the manager to make an apology to the audience for her not appearing in the dance. Quin, who looked upon all dancers 'as the mere garnish of the stage', at first demurred; but being threatened with a forfeiture, he growlingly came forward, and in his coarse way thus addressed the audience:

'Ladies and Gentlemen.'

'I am desired by the manager to inform you, that the dance intended for this night is obliged to be postponed, on account of Mademoiselle Rollan having dislocated her ankle: I wish it had been her neck, the b——ch.'

The Scots Magazine, April 1788

Mrs Pitt *1721–1799*

An actress, 'very much confined in her talents'.

Peevish characters of every kind, but particularly those of antiquated virginity, were always so well represented by her.

The Gentleman's Magazine, January 1799

Christopher Lowe *died 1801*

At Chester, aged 92, Christopher Lowe, many years bill-distributor for the Theatre Royal of Chester. This venerable patriarch was a native of Preston; and, when in his 16th year, was afflicted with a fever, of which he apparently died. He was laid out, shrowded, and coffined; and, nearly three days after his supposed demise, while carrying on four men's shoulders to the grave, he suddenly knocked at the lid of the coffin; and to the ineffable amazement of the carriers and attendants, on opening it, they found honest Christopher in a complete state of resuscitation. For many years after he used to amuse and astonish his neighbours and friends with the 'wonderful things he saw in a trance.'

The Gentleman's Magazine, April 1801

Mr Wild *died 1801*

At Liverpool, in his 52nd year, Mr. Wild, upwards of 20 years prompter of Covent-garden theatre. He was a well-informed man independent of his dramatic knowledge, which was rather extensive. As a prompter he was assiduous, diligent, and impartial, never improperly absent from his post, and equally attentive to the highest and lowest performer. In the earlier part of his life he tried the profession of an actor; but not being able to execute his own conceptions of theatrical merit, he renounced the sock and buskin, and was content to assist others in a pursuit for which he did not deem himself sufficiently qualified, though Nature had given him a good person and a solid understanding.

The Gentleman's Magazine, August 1801

John Philip Kemble 1757–1823

For eight years manager of the Drury Lane Theatre and brother of Sarah Siddons, Kemble was a founder of the declamatory school of acting.

He combined in an eminent degree the physical and mental requisites for the highest rank in his profession. To a noble form and classical and expressive countenance, he added the advantages of a sound judgement, indefatigable industry, and an ardent love and decided genius for the art of which he was so distinguished an ornament. He possessed besides, what we have always regarded as an essential characteristic of a first-rate tragic actor, an air of intellectual superiority, and a peculiarity of manner and appearance, which impressed the spectator at the first glance, with the conviction that he was not of the race of common men. His voice was defective in the undertones necessary for soliloquies; but in declamation it was strong and efficient; and in tones of melancholy indescribably touching. No music was ever heard which could better revive the tale of past times.

The Gentleman's Magazine, March 1823

Monsieur Garnerin died 1823

In Paris, M. Garnerin, the aeronaut. About a week before, he had a sudden stroke of apoplexy in the Théâtre du Jardin Beaujon, in consequence of which he let go the rope of the curtain, which was in his hand, and the curtain fell on his head and severely wounded him. From the effects of this blow he never recovered.

M. Garnerin, though perhaps not the most scientific, was one of the most adventurous aeronauts that ever dared 'With wings not given to man t'attempt the air.' He was the man who first made the experiment of descending in a parachute, and the British metropolis saw, with fear and astonishment, a daring individual, at an immeasurable distance from the earth, separating himself from the hazardous balloon to take the chance of reaching the ground in safety by an untried experiment. This event took place on the 21st of September, 1802, from an inclosure near North Audley-street.

The Gentleman's Magazine, Supplement to 1823

Sarah Siddons *1755–1831*

Born into the theatrical family of Kembles, Mrs Siddons was an infant prodigy, and a precocious beauty. Coupled with her obvious talent for acting, these brought her admiration from an early age. The dispute over her funeral arrangements, described below, was resolved by her family who wanted a 'quiet' funeral and so on 19 June she was buried in the graveyard of St Mary's, Paddington. Notwithstanding her family's wishes, five thousands admirers attended the ceremony.

To The Editor of The Times

Sir, – Mrs. Siddons is dead! Such a genius should be buried in public state.

It appears to me, that all great geniuses who have contributed to the intellectual delight of their country are entitled to such an honour. Why is it confined to statesmen or warriors? Are they the only benefactors to a nation? But I fear the English have but two passions, viz – politics and commerce – and are not yet prepared to reverence the naked majority of genius, independent of title, rank, property, power or office.

A greater genius than Mrs. Siddons in her calling never lived. She was in private life the best of mothers; pious and good in her feelings and readily bore testimony to the genius of others. To her connexions her loss is irreparable.

ALPHA
The Times, 9 June 1831

We have inserted a letter signed 'Alpha' on the death of Mrs. Siddons and let his suggestion of a public funeral have what influence it may, we shall venture our opinion on the subject. From the praise of Mrs. Siddons in her private character, we have no authority for dissenting; we therefore readily believe, even on an anonymous statement, all that is said in this

206

respect, and offer to her memory the tribute of respect for her virtues while living. But we will at the same time fearlessly assert, that there is nothing in the art of a stage-player that should entitle the most successful professor of it to a public funeral. The fact is, that we perfectly coincide with Rousseau's opinion, who, in reply to a celebrated article in the *Encyclopédie* 'on the Stage', clearly proves, at least to our satisfaction, with his own marvellous and seductive eloquence, that in a barbarous state of society the theatre is useless; in one moderately corrupt, it may render some service; but in a pure one it is prejudicial.

Besides, what is the art of a stage-player? A contingent and dependent one. How few actors have been tolerable writers. And if others did not write, they could not act. Whatever marks of private friendship, therefore, may be paid to Mrs. Siddons on her sustaining the lot of mortality, and we hope she will have many, we should consider any public testimony of regard as a proof of the decline of noble feeling in the nation, — as an evidence of its approach to that state in which *panis et circenses* were all that was thought necessary for a people.

The Times, 9 June 1831

William Charles Macready *1793–1873*

In 1845 Edwin Forrest, the American actor, visited London. His performance was not well received and he charged the successful British actor, William Charles Macready, with hiring roughs to drive him from the stage and encouraging the press to publish critical reviews. When, in 1849, Macready arrived in New York to play Macbeth at the Astor Opera House, Forrest was cast in the same rôle at the Broadway Theatre just a short distance away. Macready's performance, as related in his obituary some years later, ended in a rather surprising manner.

> The jealousy of Mr. Forrest, the actor, led to a desperate riot at the Astor Opera House, at New York, in which he was performing, when he was attacked by the mob, and with difficulty escaped with his life. The military were called out to suppress the disturbance, and having fired, killed twenty-two men on the spot, besides seriously wounding thirty others.
>
> *The Annual Register of the year 1873*

On entre, on crie,
Et c'est la vie;
On crie, on sort,
Et c'est la mort.

Anon

INDEX